# Thematic Uni

# Color

*Written by Cheryl Russell*
*Illustrated by Sue Fullam*

***Teacher Created Materials, Inc.***
P.O. Box 1040
Huntington Beach, CA 92647

Made in U.S.A.

**ISBN-1-55734-279-2**

# Table of Contents



 

# Introduction

*Color* is a literature-based thematic unit designed to teach and reinforce color concepts, encourage students to talk and write about ideas and feelings, explore the colorful world of science, introduce classroom art projects and relate the importance of color in cultures, celebrations, and holidays. Students see color everywhere, and yet they can be guided to experience it in many new ways. The unit begins with activities based on the re-illustrated book, *Hailstones and Halibut Bones*. This book features twelve beautiful poems for each of these colors: purple, gold, black, brown, blue, gray, white, orange, red, pink, green, and yellow. Included in this unit is a variety of activities in Language Arts, Math, Science, Social Studies, Art, and Music, allowing students to truly experience the world of colors. To complete this resource, there will be ideas for bulletin boards and a simple positive reinforcement program for classroom management.

This thematic unit includes:

- ❑ **Literature selections**—summaries of children's books with related lessons (complete with reproducible pages) that cross the curriculum
- ❑ **Language experience and writing ideas**—suggestions as well as activities across the curriculum, including Big Books
- ❑ **Bulletin board ideas**—suggestions and plans for student-created and/or interactive bulletin boards
- ❑ **Homework suggestions**—extending the unit to the child's home
- ❑ **Curriculum connections**—in language arts, math, science, art, music, and life skills such as cooking and physical education
- ❑ **Group projects**—to foster cooperative learning
- ❑ **Culminating activities**—which require students to synthesize their learning to produce a product or engage in an activity that can be shared with others
- ❑ **Bibliography**—suggesting additional literature and nonfiction books on the theme

To keep this valuable resource intact so it can be used year after year, you may wish to punch holes in the pages and store them in a three-ring binder.

# Introduction *(cont.)*

## Why Whole Language?

A whole language approach involves children in using all modes of communication: reading, writing, listening, observing, illustrating, experiencing, and doing. Communication skills are interconnected and integrated into lessons that emphasize the whole of language rather than isolating its parts. The lessons revolve around selected literature. Reading is not taught as a separate subject from writing and spelling, for example. A child reads, writes (spelling appropriately for his/her level), speaks, listens, etc., in response to a literature experience introduced by the teacher. In this way, language skills grow naturally, stimulated by involvement and interest in the topic at hand.

## Why Thematic Planning?

One very useful tool for implementing an integrated whole language program is thematic planning. By choosing a theme with correlative literature selections for a unit of study, a teacher can plan activities throughout the day that lead to a cohesive, in-depth study of the topic. Students will be practicing and applying their skills in meaningful contexts. Consequently, they will tend to learn and retain more. Both teachers and students will be freed from a day that is broken into unrelated segments of isolated drill and practice.

## Why Cooperative Learning?

Besides academic skills and content, students need to learn social skills. No longer can this area of development be taken for granted. Students must learn to work cooperatively in groups in order to function well in modern society. Group activities should be a regular part of school life, and teachers should consciously include social objectives as well as academic objectives in their planning. For example, a group working together to solve a problem may need to select a leader. The teacher should make clear to the students and monitor the qualities of good leader-follower group interaction just as he/she would state and monitor the academic goals of the project.

## Why Big Books?

An excellent cooperative whole language activity is the production of Big Books. Groups of students, or the whole class, can apply their language skills, content knowledge, and creativity to produce a Big Book that can become a part of the classroom library to be read and reread. These books make excellent culminating projects for sharing beyond the classroom with parents, librarians, other classes, etc. Big Books can be produced in many ways, and this thematic unit book includes directions for at least one method you may choose.

 

# *Hailstones and Halibut Bones*

## *by Mary O'Neill (Doubleday, 1961)*

*(Available in Canada from Doubleday Dell Seal; in the U.K. from U.K. Doubleday/Bantam Dell; and in Australia from Transworld Publishers.)*

### Summary

Hailstones and Halibut Bones *is a collection of twelve poems about colors: black, red, blue, yellow, green, orange, purple, gold, white, pink, brown, and gray. Color is known best by sight. These delightful poems reveal that color is connected with other senses of sound, smell, taste, and touch. This classic book of poetry presents ideal material for exploring the world of color.*

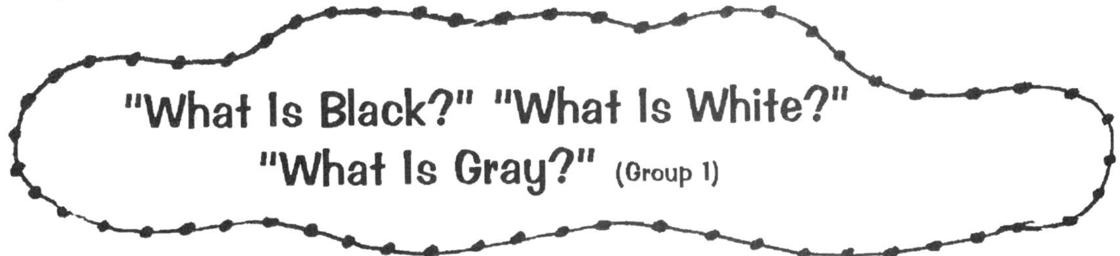


The outline below is a suggested plan for using the various activities that are presented in this unit. You should adapt these ideas to fit your classroom situation.

## Sample Plan

### Day 1

- Literature selection (page 34) *Winnie the Witch*
- Color Mixing art project (page 55)
- Book Corner (page 6, Setting the Stage #1)
- Send parent letter home. (page 71)
- Introduce *Hailstones and Halibut Bones.*
- Read "What Is Black?" "What Is White?" "What Is Gray?"
- Discussion (page 6, Enjoying the Poems #1)
- Be a Detective worksheet (page 8)

### Day 2

- Re-read poems using props. (page 33)
- Rhyme exercise (page 6, Enjoying the Poems #2)
- Literature Selection (page 34) *White is the Moon*
- Read *Rainbow Crow* and discuss value of storytelling. (page 7, #1)
- Storytelling worksheet for homework (page 45)
- "Air Pollution" fact sheet (page 52)
- "Pollution Solution" homework (page 53)
- Hidden Pollution (page 54)
- Picture Match (page 10)
- Classroom Fun activities (page 73)
- Colorful Senses worksheet (page 12)

### Day 3

- Share *Rainbow Crow* storytelling.
- Newspaper activity (page 46)
- Make newspaper hats. (page 7, #9)
- Hand prints for bulletin board (page 72)
- Math Story worksheet (page 11)
- Play Word Scramble Run. (page 58)
- Classroom Fun activity (page 73)
- Discuss Solutions to Pollution ideas.
- Arrange bulletin board.

# Overview of Activities

## Setting the Stage

1. Set up a book corner. Make it a comfortable place to be. Collect books where color is the theme (See bibliography page 79 for suggestions.) Provide time for the children to look at and read these books on their own. Adult volunteers or older students may help those who cannot read yet, but all children will enjoy the pictures.
2. Letting parents know about the unit on colors will enable them to participate with their children on some of the assignments. Have children color the parent letter on page 71 before sending it home.
3. Help children think about the following colors: black, white, and gray. Cut an equal number of squares out of black, white, and gray construction paper, enough for each child. Put them in a bag and have the children pick out a square. This will put the class into three groups. Allow time for the groups to think of things that match the color of their square. Share their findings with the class.
4. Have pictures or actual items of things ready to illustrate the first group of poems from *Hailstones and Halibut Bones.* See page 33 for a checklist of props.
5. Introduce the book, *Hailstones and Halibut Bones.* Show the book cover. Tell the children that the book has 12 poems in it about colors. Have them guess what colors the author is going to write about.

## Enjoying the Poems

1. Read each of the three poems for the colors of black, white, and gray. Encourage the children to participate in the poems by holding the items or pictures that you have collected as they are mentioned. After you have finished reading the poems, ask the following questions to help the children further explore these colors:
   1. Of the three colors, which do you like best and why?
   2. Was there anything mentioned that you did not know was that color?
   3. Are gray and black similar? Black and white? White and gray?
   4. What does "Black is kind" mean? What is the sound of black?
   5. Why is white "out of touch" or "out of sight"?
   6. How would you feel if there were no colors except black, white, and gray?
2. Re-read the poems and allow the children to respond. For example, in "What Is Black?" begin with "Black is the night when there isn't a ____ and you can't tell by looking where you ____." This will help children with the rhythm of the poem as well as the contents.
3. Do Color Mixing worksheet on page 55.
4. Classroom Fun on page 73 will give you some ideas for clothing days and exercise breaks.

 

# Overview of Activities *(cont.)*

## Extending the Poems

1. *Rainbow Crow* (see bibliography, page 79) is a legend of how the crow became black in color. It comes from the Lenape Native American tribe and has been handed down from generation to generation.

   Read the story and discuss the value of storytelling. Have students talk with their families and record a story (see page 45). Younger children may draw pictures to help them re-tell the story to the class. Suggestions for storytelling topics could include a favorite recipe, a relative, a family tradition, a cultural practice, or an heirloom.

   Collect the stories (or artwork) and make a book of them.

2. Refer to Literature Ideas for suggested reading (see page 34).
3. Introduce "Be a Detective" worksheets on pages 8 and 9 with the theme music from the *Pink Panther*. Have a magnifying glass available to help children understand they are looking for clues.
4. Do "Picture Match" activity sheet on page 10.
5. Play Word Scramble Run (page 58).
6. Gray is associated with the color of smog. Read the "Air Pollution" fact sheet on page 52. Involve the children in ideas for cleaning up the environment with the worksheet on page 53 and Hidden Pollution activity on page 54. Make a bulletin board with their ideas and pledges.
7. Do Math Story worksheet (page 11).
8. In addition to sight, colors represent smell, taste, touch, and sound. Colorful Senses on page 12 will help children to understand how colors relate to all five senses.
9. "What's black and white and read all over?" is a riddle that children have told each other for years. Use it as an introduction to study the newspaper. Ask each child to bring in a newspaper. Discuss the purpose of a newspaper. After completing the worksheet on page 46, make a newspaper hat.

Using one page of your newspaper:

1. Fold the newspaper sheet in half, from top to bottom.
2. Fold the top left and top right corners in to meet along the center line.
3. Fold the bottom edge of top sheet halfway up. Then fold it up again. Turn it over and do the same thing to the other side.
4. Now you have a newspaper hat!

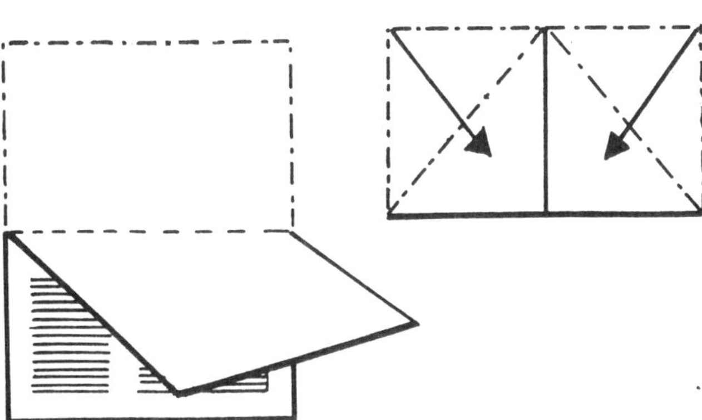

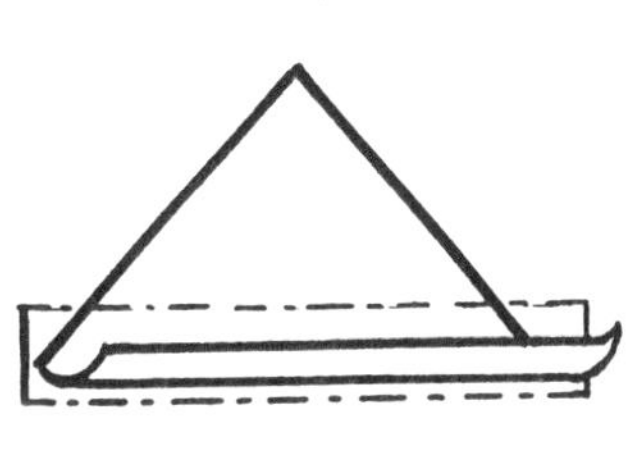

Name ________________________________

# Be a Detective

In the book of poems, *Hailstones and Halibut Bones,* many things were described in black, white, and gray. Be a detective and name three for each color.

**Black**

1. ________________________

2. ________________________

3. ________________________

**White**

1. ________________________

2. ________________________

3. ________________________

**Gray**

1. ________________________

2. ________________________

3. ________________________

 

Name ______________________________

# Be a Detective *(cont.)*

Identify the pictures by writing the correct color:

| Black | White | Gray |
|---|---|---|

______________ ______________ ______________

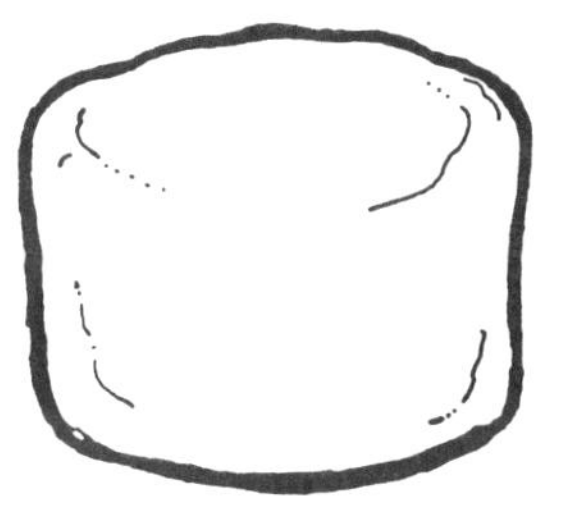

______________ ______________ ______________

______________ ______________ ______________

**Name** ______________________________________________

# Picture Match

Some things can be more than one color. Look at the pictures below and draw an arrow to the center box if it is possible for the picture to be colored all three of these colors: black, gray, and white.

Name ______________________________

# Math Story

Solve each problem. Read the sentences below. The missing word is spelled by matching the correct answer with the letter next to it.

| | | |
|---|---|---|
| 3 + 1 = _____ (A) | 8- 2 = _____ (B) | 12 + 2 = _____ (C) |
| 6 + 4 = _____ (E) | 7- 5 = _____ (S) | 9- 8 = _____ (N) |
| 7- 4 = _____ (O) | 4 + 5 = _____ (K) | 11- 6 = _____ (L) |
| 2 + 5 = _____ (F) | 8 + 5 = _____ (M) | 6 + 5 = _____ (U) |
| | 4 + 4 = _____ (W) | |

Complete each sentence below.

1. A ___ ___ ___ ___ ___ ___ ___ ___ ___ is white.
   (2 1 3 8 7 5 4 9 10)

2. The gray ___ ___ ___ ___ ___ ate all the cheese.
   (13 3 11 2 10)

3. ___ ___ ___ ___ whales are large mammals.
   (6 5 11 10)

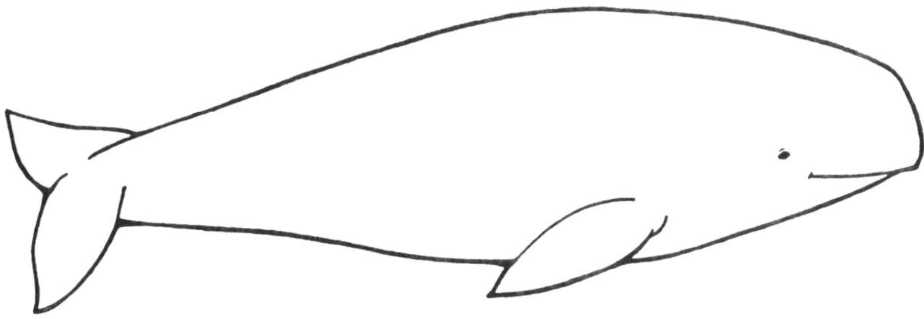

Name ______________________________

# Colorful Senses

There are 5 senses: sight, sound, smell, taste, and touch. The colors black, white, and gray are the easiest to see. These colors can also be described by other senses.

Label each sentence with the correct sense: **sight, sound, smell, taste, or touch.**

1. Black is "boom, boom, boom!" ______________
2. Gray is smoke swirls. ______________
3. White is light foot walking. ______________
4. Black is a smokestack. ______________
5. Gray is chewing gum. ______________
6. White is whispers talking. ______________
7. Black is licorice. ______________
8. Gray is velvety. ______________
9. White is a cherry bloom. ______________

On the back of this page, draw a picture. Include an example of each sense.

 

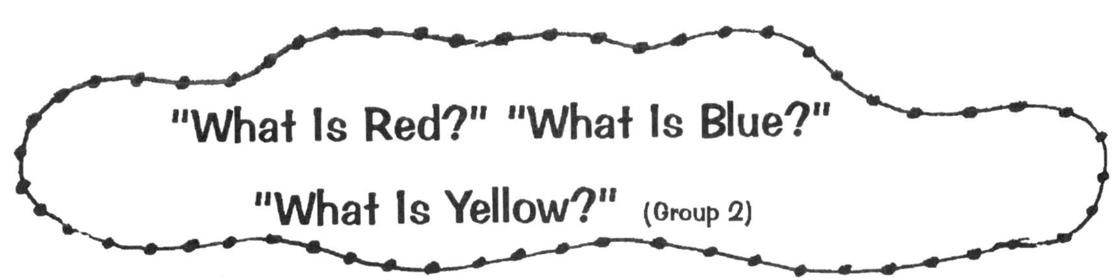

# "What Is Red?" "What Is Blue?" "What Is Yellow?" (Group 2)

The outline below is a suggested plan for using the various activities that are presented in this unit. You should adapt these ideas to fit your classroom situation.

## Sample Plan

**Day 1**

- Book Corner (#1 below)
- Classroom Fun (page 73)
- Invite printing representatives to speak.
- Read "What is Red?" "What is Blue?" "What is Yellow?"
- Discuss poems.
- How Many Blue Eyes? worksheet (page 15)
- Red Cross/First Aid worksheet (pages 48 & 49)
- Rhyme Time worksheet (page 16)
- Journal Writing—Red (pages 35 & 36)

**Day 2**

- Literature selection (page 34)
- Journal Writing—Blue (pages 35 & 36)
- Hand prints for bulletin board (page 72)
- Bullseye worksheet (page 17)
- Flower Colors worksheet (page 18)
- Classroom Fun (page 73)
- The Blue Sea (page 50)
- Color your number. (page 44)
- Colorful Oceans Scenes (page 51)
- Making butter (page 62)
- Corn feast (page 62)

**Day 3**

- Classroom Fun (page 73)
- Journal Writing—Yellow (pages 35 & 37)
- History in Color worksheet (page 19)
- Uniforms worksheet (page 47)
- Popcorn game (page 59)
- Red, Blue, Yellow potluck (page 14, #7)
- Choral activity (page 14, Extending the Poems, #1)

## Overview of Activities

### Setting the Stage

1. Remind the students of the book corner. Be sure to point out the particular books that relate to Group 2 colors. Some suggested titles are: *Colors Red, Colors Blue, Colors Yellow; Is it Red? Is it Yellow? Is it Blue?; Who Said Red?; One Yellow Lion.*

2. Do some Classroom Fun activities. (See page 73.)

3. Invite a representative from a printing company to visit your class. Printing is a combination of four colors: red (magenta), blue, yellow, and black. Ask the person to bring samples of each color negative, pages run with one color, two colors, three colors, and four colors. This will be an excellent demonstration. If this is not possible, a simple book that will help you explain the four-color process is *How a Book is Made* by Aliki.

4. Collect props for reading the poems. (See page 33.)

# Overview of Activities *(cont.)*

## Enjoying the Poems

1. Read the poems: "What is Red?" "What is Blue?" and "What is Yellow?"
2. Discuss the following questions to help children see the range of these colors:
   * Why does feeling embarrassed make your face red?
   * How many things can you name that are blue?
   * What does blue sound like? red? yellow?
   * What are the fun feelings of yellow?
   * What is your favorite thing in yellow? red? blue?
3. A worksheet called "How Many Blue Eyes?" will help the children with fractions. Divide the class in groups of two for the first exercise, up to six in a group for the last exercise. (See page 15.)
4. Rhyme Time reinforces the sounds of the words red, blue, and yellow. (See page 16.)
5. Flowers are associated with color. See page 18 for Flower Colors worksheet.
6. Try the journal writing exercises on pages 35-37.

## Extending the Poems

1. The book *Who Said Red?* makes a fun oral language activity. Have the words to the story typed for distribution to each child. Divide the class into four groups. You are the narrator. Begin reading *Who Said Red?* and let the first group answer about red. When they ask, "Did you say red?" you respond, "Yes, I said red!" The next group reads the green part and again you respond with "No, I said red!" Continue through the book to the end. Children will love the question and answer rhythm.
2. Do the Bullseye Math worksheet on page 17.
3. Complete the History in Color worksheet on page 19.
4. A universal symbol is the red cross. This represents help and first aid. Two worksheets, "What Does Red Cross Mean?" and "Safety and First Aid" can be found on pages 48-49.
5. "Blue is the quiet sea" comes from the poem, "What is Blue?" You may want to use this as a lead in for an extensive unit on the study of the ocean. Have children do the color by numbers that reveals a sea animal in the ocean on page 50. Also, have students make a colorful ocean scene. (See page 51.)
6. Use the book, *Colors Blue,* to lead a discussion about uniforms that come in blue—the U.S. Navy, British policemen, blue collar workers, and even jeans are used for some types of jobs. See page 47 for a follow-up worksheet.
7. Plan a red, blue, and yellow potluck. Have each child bring a food item and set up a potluck table for snack time. Suggestions include: bananas, raspberries, cherries, blueberries, tomatoes, lemonade, lemon pudding, watermelon, and pineapple.

 

Name ____________________________________________

# How Many Blue Eyes?

**Directions:**

- Divide the class into groups of two.
- In groups of two, ask how many children have blue eyes.
- Place the number in the space provided.

  **Example:** if one child has blue eyes, place a one in the space provided. $\frac{1}{2}$
- Repeat for groups of three, four, five and six.

**Groups of 2**

How many have blue eyes? ________

What fraction of the group has blue eyes? $\frac{\_\_\_}{2}$

**Groups of 3**

How many have blue eyes? ________

What fraction of the group has blue eyes? $\frac{\_\_\_}{3}$

**Groups of 4**

How many have blue eyes? ________

What fraction of the group has blue eyes? $\frac{\_\_\_}{4}$

**Groups of 5**

How many have blue eyes? ________

What fraction of the group has blue eyes? $\frac{\_\_\_}{5}$

**Groups of 6**

How many have blue eyes? ________

What fraction of the group has blue eyes? $\frac{\_\_\_}{6}$

Name ______________________________

# Rhyme Time

Write the words listed below that rhyme with red, blue, and yellow.

**Blue** ______________________________

______________________________

______________________________

**Red** ______________________________

______________________________

______________________________

**Yellow** ______________________________

______________________________

______________________________

| | | | | | |
|---|---|---|---|---|---|
| glue | head | bed | fellow | flew | zoo |
| mellow | you | too | shed | said | jello |
| | fled | bellow | few | dead | |

Name ________________________________________

# Bullseye

Add. Answer the questions. Color the bullseye.

2+3 =

9+1 =

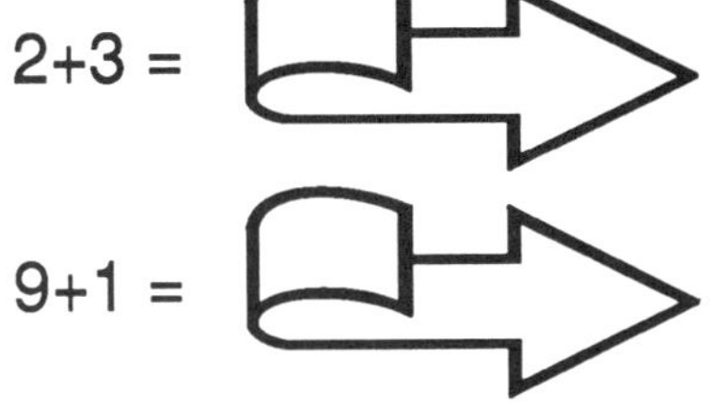

6+9 =

5+0 = 

7+8 =

7+3 =

8+2 =

5+5 = 

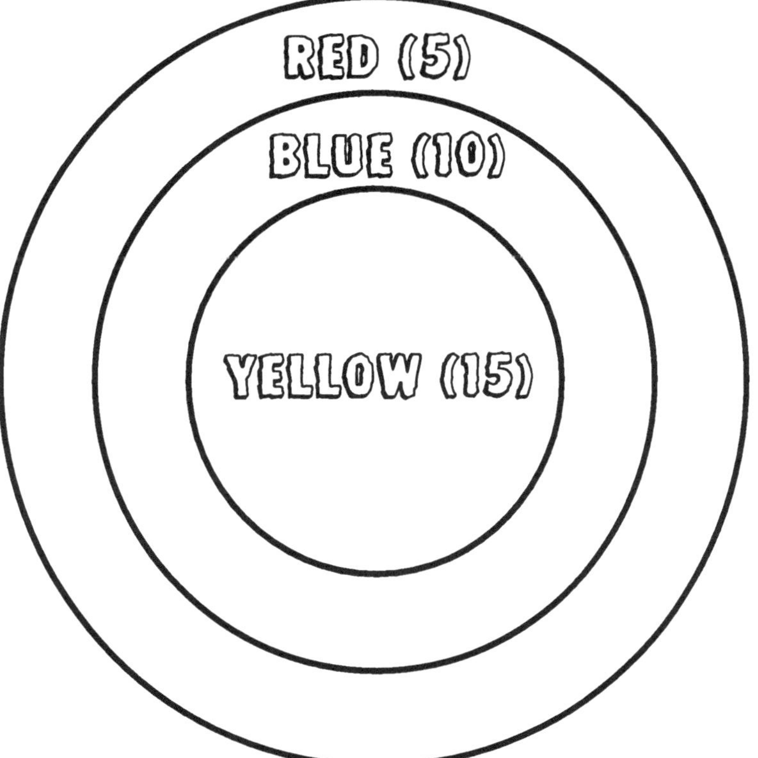


1. How many arrows landed on the red? ____________________
2. How many arrows landed on the blue? ____________________
3. How many arrows landed on the yellow? ____________________
4. Which color has the most arrows? ____________________
5. Which color has the least arrows? ____________________

**Name** ______________________________

# Flower Colors

1. Color the flowers correctly according to the poems.

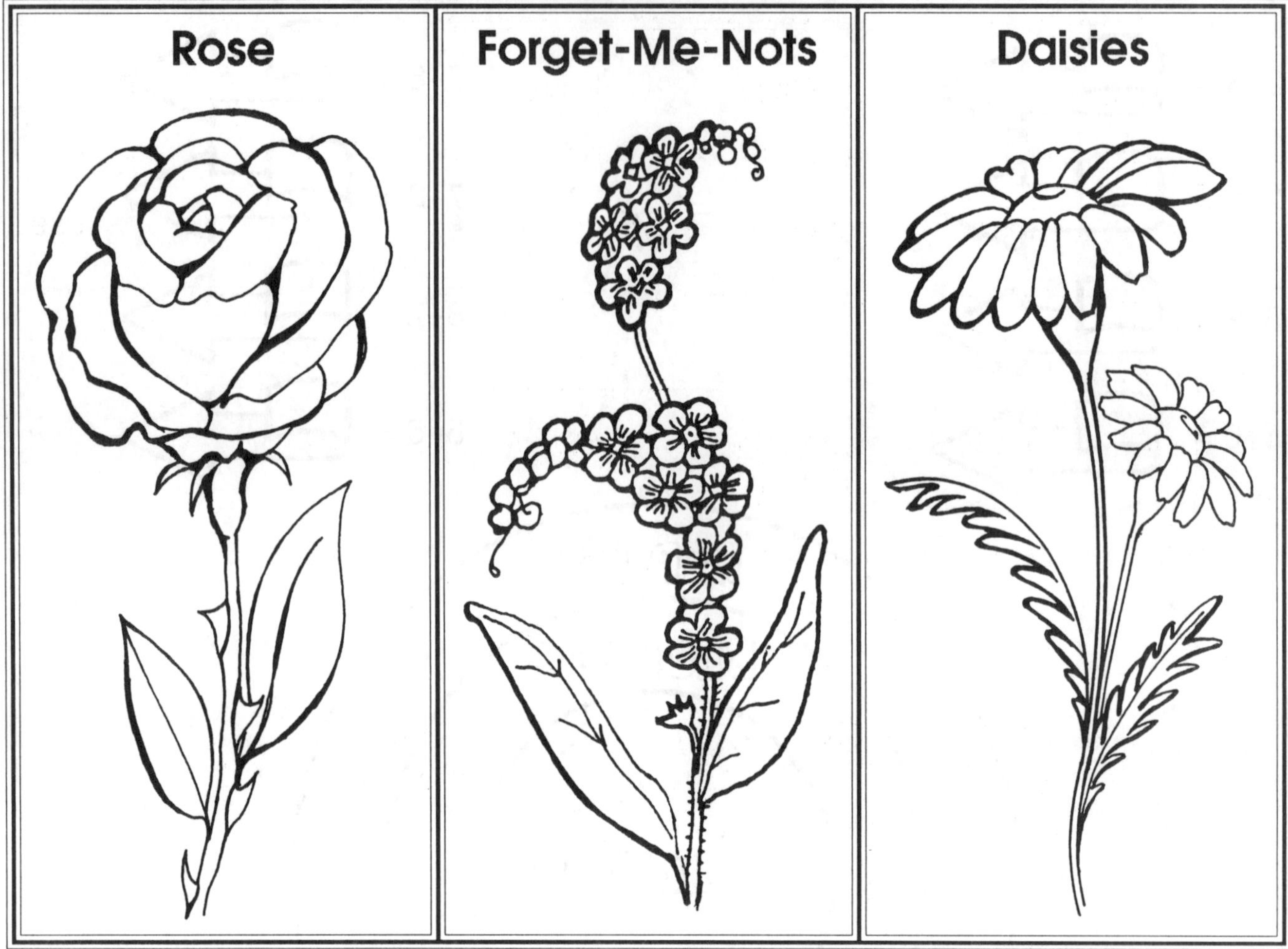


2. My favorite flower is: ______________________________

   because ______________________________

   I picked this flower for you because ______________________________

   ______________________________

   ______________________________

   ______________________________

3. Cut out your favorite flower and make a card.
4. Use your explanation for the greeting.
5. Give it to someone special.

 

Name ________________________________________

# History in Color

Find the correct color to identify famous events. Choose from:

| White | Gold | Blue | Yellow | Gray | Red |
|---|---|---|---|---|---|

1. The President of the United States lives in the ________________ House.
2. A lot of people moved to California during the ____________________ rush.
3. British soldiers were called the ________________ coats.
4. Another name for the flag of the United States is the ______________, ______________,and ______________.
5. Many soldiers died during the Spanish-American War from an illness known as ______________ fever.

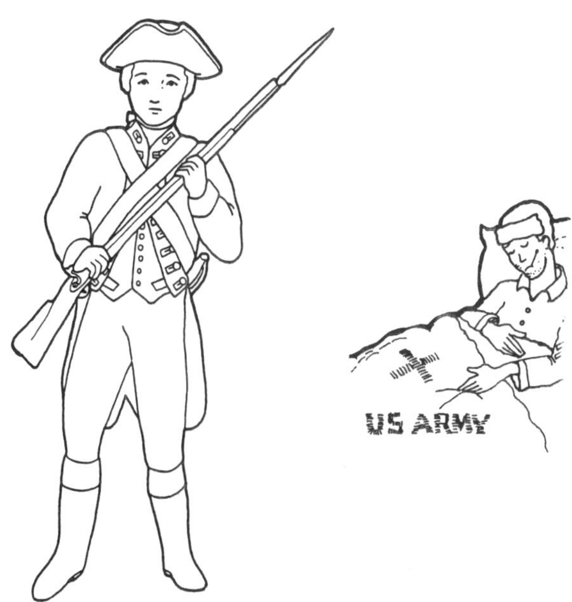

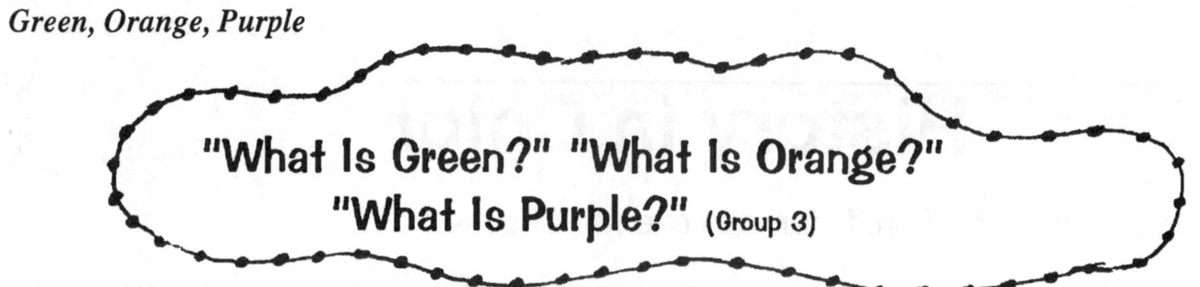


The outline below is a suggested plan for using the various activities that are presented in this unit. You should adapt these ideas to fit your classroom situation.

## Sample Plan

### Day 1

- Literature selection (page 34)
- Book Corner (#1 below)
- Floral arrangement (#3 below)
- Read "What Is Green?" "What Is Orange?" "What Is Purple?"
- Discussion (page 21, Enjoying the Poems #2)
- Classroom Fun (page 73)
- Make a Collage (page 22)
- Journal Writing—Green (pages 35, 37)
- Balloon Volleyball (page 59)

### Day 2

- Hidden Colors activity (page 24)
- Feelings About Colors Survey (page 42)
- Green, Orange, Purple snacks (page 21, Enjoying the Poems #3)
- Art Color Wheel (page 56)
- Classroom Fun (page 73)
- Journal Writing—Orange (page 38)

### Day 3

- Classroom Fun (page 73)
- Graph Math Survey (page 43)
- Maypole Dancing (page 21, Extending the Poems #4)
- Write Songs (page 21, Extending the Poems #4)
- Make Maypoles (page 21, Extending the Poems #4)
- Classroom Management (pages 74-78)
- Journal Writing—Purple (page 38)
- Word Scramble (page 25)
- Can You Hear Color? (page 21, Extending the Poems #5)
- Hand Prints for Bulletin Board (page 72)

# Overview of Activities

## Setting the Stage

1. Remind students of the book corner. Be sure to point out the particular books that relate to Group 3 colors: *Planting a Rainbow; Hawaii is a Rainbow; Harold and the Purple Crayon; Colors Green.*
2. Use the Classroom Fun activities. (See page 73).
3. Since this group features flowers and greenery, create a floral arrangement out of real flowers or pictures if they are not available in your area. Silk or artificial flowers could also be used. Include in your arrangement flowers and greenery from the poems: ivy, greenery, marigolds, and tiger lilies.
4. Collect props for reading poems. (See page 33).

 

# Overview of Activities *(cont.)*

## Enjoying the Poems

1. Read the poems: "What Is Green?" "What Is Orange?" and "What Is Purple?"
2. Use these questions for class discussion:
   * Why is April green? What are the signs of spring?
   * What is the holiday for wearing green?
   * What colors are in a sunset? How about dawn?
   * Is orange the brightest color?
   * Is purple more popular than you think?
   * What colors are similar to purple? Very different?

3. Have fruit snacks of orange slices and grapes (green and purple).
4. Refer to the literature ideas (page 34) for suggested reading and write about the colors in the journal writing activity (see pages 37-38)
5. Make a Collage activity. (See page 22.)
6. Children will enjoy having fun with the words green, orange, and purple in Hidden Colors (page 24) and Word Scramble (page 25).

## Extending the Poems

1. Children will have an opportunity to see how primary colors mix together making green, orange, and purple. The Color Wheel activity on page 56 can be added to their journal books.
2. Since the children are using journals to write their feelings about colors, making a survey will be a fun extension. Cut squares of red, blue, yellow, green, orange, and purple out of construction paper for each child. Instruct the children to show the squares, one at a time, to at least 10 people. Have them record which of the four feelings the person "feels" from the color they were shown (warm, hot, cool, or cold). See page 42. When the children have the results of their survey, total the findings and have each child make a graph of the results. (See page 43.)
3. Classroom management programs are important to the success of learning and positive behavior. See pages 74-78 for a complete description of a classroom program that utilizes colors, positive reinforcement, individual rewards, and class incentives.
4. Make a Maypole by attaching long strips of cloth or crepe paper streamers to a pole or a trunk of a tree. Add flowers and colorful bows for decoration. As an indoor activity, a long tube anchored in clay will work nicely.

   May Day is celebrated around the Maypole on May 1st. Maypoles can be fun any time of the year. Have the students write simple songs about colors using tunes they know. For example: "Twinkle, twinkle little star. What is your color from afar? I am red, that's what I said. I am blue, what about you?"
5. Can you hear color? Using available musical instruments, have students wearing green compose a song that represents green. Those wearing other colors will compose songs about their colors.
6. Students now have the opportunity to write their own poems about color. Reproduce enough pages for students to create several poems. Encourage them to try some color poems without using the frame. Have the students use the cover provided or have them design their own. Allow the students to share the books orally with the class. (See pages 40-41.)
7. A physically fun activity called "Balloon Volleyball" is a sure hit. (See page 59.)

Name ______________________________

# Make a Collage

A collage is a collection of pictures, photographs, drawings, or scenes. Usually a collage has a theme such as family pictures, school days, or sports.

The poems in *Hailstones and Halibut Bones* suggest pictures in green, orange, and purple.

Color, cut, and paste these pictures on a piece of construction paper to make a collage. You may wish to draw or cut some pictures out of a magazine to add to your collage.

Name ________________________________________

# Bear Parade

Color one row of bears green, one row orange, and one row purple. Cut out the bears and arrange them in a pattern.

Name ________________________________

# Hidden Colors

In the sentences below, each of the color words is hidden. Find the hidden color word and circle it. Write the color word on the line next to the sentence.

| | |
|---|---|
| **black** | **red** |
| **green** | **orange** |
| **gray** | **purple** |
| **yellow** | **white** |

**Example:** Are donkeys really stubborn? **red**

1. The taxicab lacks a tire. ____________

2. The boy will yell "ow" when he fails. ____________

3. The cow hit every fly with her tail. ____________

4. Will you take out the spur, please? ____________

5. Fred goes to school with his brother. ____________

6. The grouchy ogre enjoyed himself. ____________

7. Color angels so they can be seen. ____________

8. Where are you going, Ray? ____________

 

Name ______________________________________________

# Word Scramble

Find each of these words three times in the puzzle: green, orange and purple. Circle each word using the appropriate color crayon.

V G M W P B G O G R E E N O

L F U Z U O P U R P L E F R

Z T C G R E E N E A S D F A

N X L A P N X O E Z Q O G N

B C N E L B Y T N A V P E G

R G P Q E S A B O R A N G E

E D J T I Z K N P U R P L E

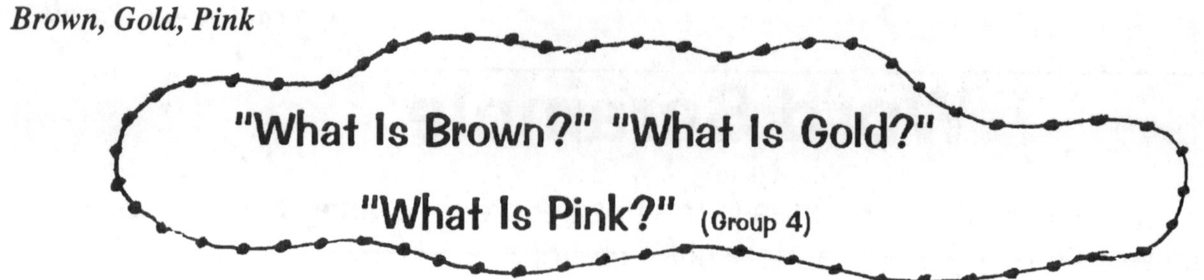

# "What Is Brown?" "What Is Gold?" "What Is Pink?" (Group 4)

The outline below is a suggested plan for using the various activities that are presented in this unit. You should adapt these ideas to fit your classroom situation.

## Sample Plan

### Day 1

- Literature Selection (page 34)
- Read "What is Brown?" "What is Gold?" and "What is Pink?"
- Discussion (page 27, Enjoying the Poems #2)
- Morning snacks (#5 below)
- Classroom Fun (page 73)
- Journal Writing—Gold (page 39)

### Day 2

- Journal Writing—Pink (page 39)
- Yarn Art (page 57)
- Dyeing Yarn (page 57)
- Yarn Decor (page 57)
- Yarn Stars worksheet (page 61)
- Color Your Number (page 44)
- Stardom! (page 60)
- Color Dance (page 27, Extending the Poems #1)
- Compare and Contrast (page 32)

### Days 3-5

- Hand prints for Bulletin Board (page 72)
- Homeward Bound (pages 30-31)
- Gold Coins/Count the Change (pages 28-29)
- Send home party invitations.
- Culminating Activity (pages 63-70)
- Language Arts (page 63)
- Science (page 64)
- Social Studies (page 63)
- Colorful Celebrations Party (page 70)

## Overview of Activities

### Setting the Stage

1. Remind the students of the book corner. Be sure to point out the particular books that relate to Group 4 colors: *Brown Bear, Brown Bear, What Do You See?; Goldilocks and the Three Bears.*
2. Use the Classroom Fun activities (see page 73).
3. Use pieces of cellophane to show how to create gold, brown, and pink. For example, put one sheet of red behind a sheet of white to create pink a sheet of orange and yellow to make gold, or a sheet of red and a sheet of green to make brown.
4. Collect props for reading the poems (see page 33).
5. Greet the children with a morning snack featuring foods from this color group. Decorate their tables with pink roses in little bud vases. Serve honey and peanut butter on bread squares. The recipe is on page 62.

 

# Overview of Activities *(cont.)*

## Enjoying the Poems

1. Read the poems “What Is Brown?” “What Is Gold?” and “What Is Pink?”
2. Use these questions for class discussion:

   * Of the foods that are brown, which is your favorite?
   * Why is brown the color of work?
   * Do you think of gold when you think of the moon and the stars?
   * How are gold and yellow similar? Different?
   * Why is pink the little sister of red?

3. Do Compare and Contrast Venn diagram (page 32).
4. Do Gold Coins (pages 28-29).
5. Try Scarf juggling (page 60).

## Extending the Poems

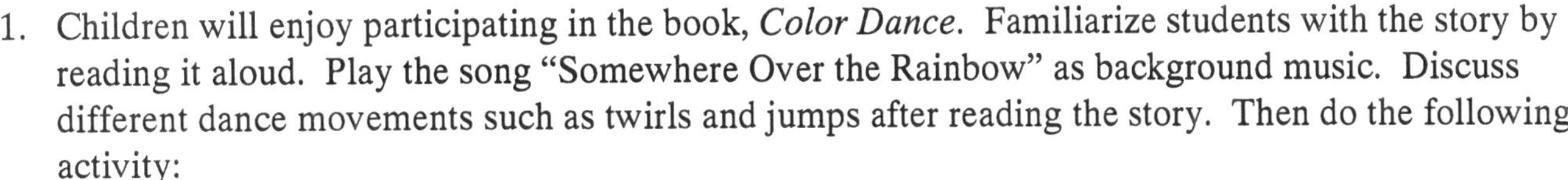

1. Children will enjoy participating in the book, *Color Dance*. Familiarize students with the story by reading it aloud. Play the song “Somewhere Over the Rainbow” as background music. Discuss different dance movements such as twirls and jumps after reading the story. Then do the following activity:

   Obtain square yard pieces of plain fabric or tissue paper for each of the fifteen colors in the story. Have students stand and practice waving their arms as if they were dancing. Now read the story, encouraging groups of students to do their own interpretation of “color dance.”

2. Yarn Art offers several activities. Children can dye their own yarn to make bracelets. Other colored yarn will make colorful room decorations just in time for the Colorful Celebrations Party. (See page 57.)
3. Stardom! will help children make stars correctly. Begin with the activity on page 61 followed by the outdoor activity described on page 60.
4. Memorizing home telephone numbers will have new meaning with the Color Your Number activity. (See page 44.)
5. Photography began in black and white. Colored film opened a whole new world. Check with local photography stores for posters from film companies. Use these as topics for writing assignments.
6. After completing the journal writing for pink, follow it up with a discussion on how to stay in the pink. Ideas for discussion are:

   • *What foods make a good breakfast?*
   • *How much sleep do you need each night?*
   • *What kind of exercise can be done?*

You may wish to have children create a poster about ways to stay healthy. Have a contest and let the class select the top three posters. Prizes could be toothbrushes, free lunch tickets, or no homework.

*Brown, Gold, Pink*

**Name** ______________________________

# Gold Coins

Directions: Color the coins gold.

Cut out.

Use the coins to count the change on the next page.

25¢ 25¢ 25¢ 25¢ 25¢

5¢ 5¢ 5¢ 5¢ 5¢

5¢ 5¢ 5¢ 5¢ 5¢

1¢ 1¢ 1¢ 1¢ 1¢ 1¢

1¢ 1¢ 1¢ 1¢ 1¢ 1¢

1¢ 1¢ 1¢ 1¢ 1¢ 1¢

 

Name ________________________________________

# Count the Change

**Directions**: Answer these questions by pasting on the correct gold coins. The leprechaun needs your help!

1. The leprechaun had 25 cents in gold coins. Show the correct change.

2. The leprechaun wants to know how many gold nickel coins equal a gold quarter coin. Show the correct number of nickels.

3. The leprechaun had 5 gold pennies. He was given 3 gold pennies. How much does he have now?

4. The leprechaun had a dollar gold piece. He bought a candy treat for 98 gold pennies. How much does he have left?

5. The leprechaun wished for 30 cents in gold coins. Show how much change he would have if his wish came true.

 

*Brown, Gold, Pink*
**Name** ________________________________________

# Homeward Bound

Study the animals below.

Draw a line to show where the animal lives.

# Home Sweet Home

Describe where you live. Try to use the words brown, gold, and pink. Draw a picture of where you live.

Name ______________________________

# Compare and Contrast

The color brown can be compared and contrasted to the color gold. In the poems from *Hailstones and Halibut Bones*, there were some common things mentioned for both gold and brown.

Place the words in the correct area to complete the diagram.

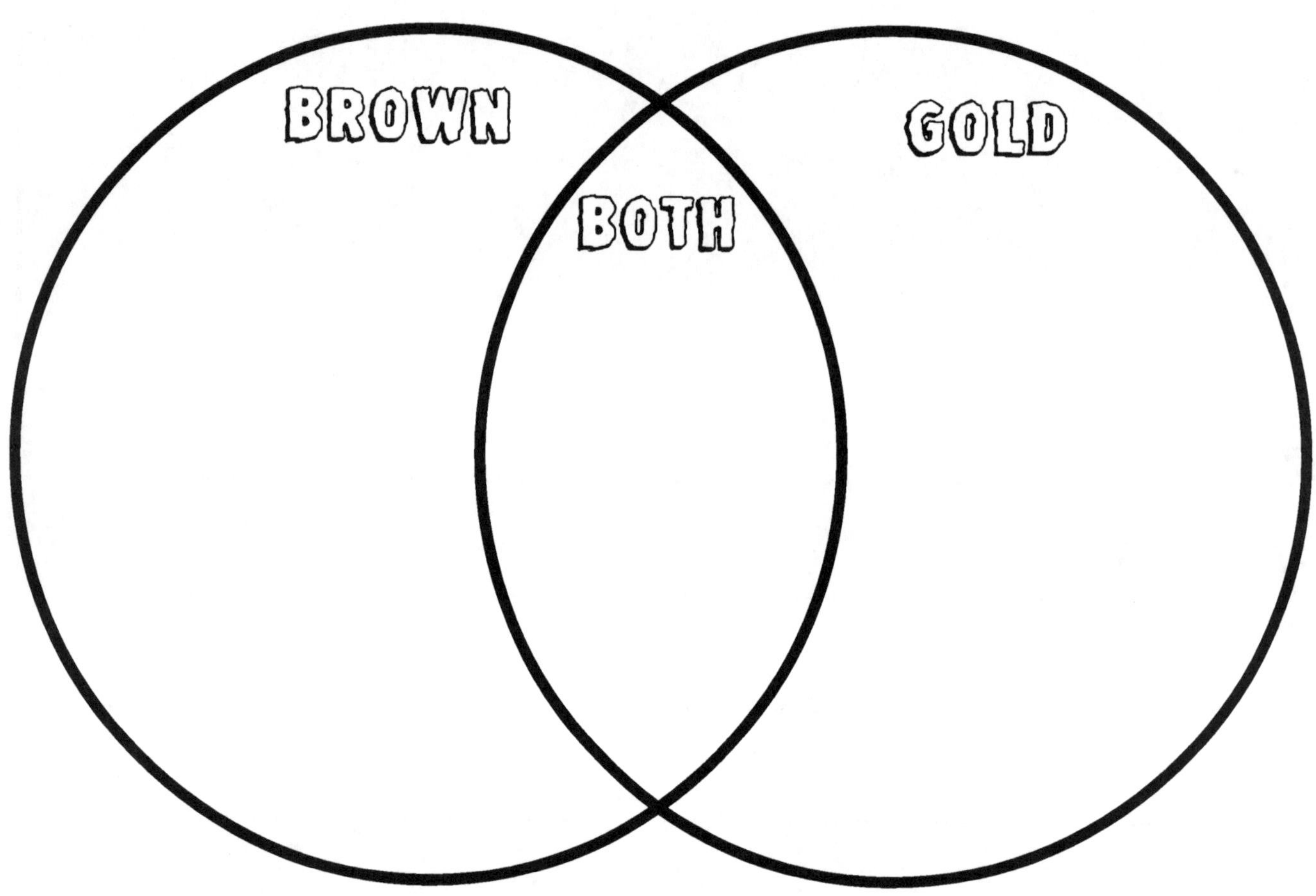


| | |
|---|---|
| **sunshine** | **metals** |
| **foods** | **stars** |
| **money** | **freckles** |
| **feelings** | **chocolate** |
| **turtles and toads** | |

 

# Props for Poems

The poems for each group are very descriptive. To help children with all the things mentioned in each poem, here is a list of props to use.

Suggestions for using the props:

* If pictures are used, display them on a flannel board.
* If using actual items, have different children hold them. When the item is mentioned in the poem, have the child stand with the prop.

## Group 1

| Black | | White | | Gray | |
|---|---|---|---|---|---|
| charcoal | licorice | dove | milk | elephant | mouse |
| newspaper | leopard | ship's sail | kite's tail | old house | fog |
| raven | black paint | telephone | marshmallow | smog | oysters |
| tar | smokestack | vanilla ice cream | lace | smoke | eagles |
| cat | black silk hat | snowflakes | | gray-haired people | nanny goats |
| patent leather shoes | | lily of the valley | | | |

## Group 2

| Red | | Blue | | Yellow | |
|---|---|---|---|---|---|
| rose | brick | sky | ocean | sun | egg yolk |
| rubber band | fire engine | scarf | sapphire | duck's bill | canary |
| heart | lipstick | heron | | corn | daisy |
| rubber ball | | forget-me-nots | | custard pie | lemon pie |
| | | | | summer squash | dandelion |

## Group 3

| Green | | Orange | | Purple | |
|---|---|---|---|---|---|
| pickle | peppermint | tiger lillies | carrots | asters | purple ink |
| elf | green grapes | sunset | marigolds | violets | nail polish |
| ivy | grass | oranges | fox | grape jelly-jam | |
| leaves | lettuce | | | | |
| moss | grasshopper | | | | |
| jade | olive | | | | |

## Group 4

| Brown | | Gold | | Pink | |
|---|---|---|---|---|---|
| turtle | toad | metal | ring | rose | seashell |
| cinnamon | toast | muffin | stars | shrimp | ribbon |
| old house | hair | honey | coins | peach blossom | |
| freckle | mole | goldfish | king's crown | Easter Bunny | |
| chocolate | gingerbread | | | | |
| leather | glove | | | | |

# Literature Ideas

There are many books focusing on color as the theme, not just an adjective. Here are brief summaries and book recommendations for each group suggested in the lesson plans.

## Group 1: *"What Is Black?" "What Is Gray?" "What Is White?"*

*Winnie the Witch* is a delightful story about a witch who lives in a house where everything is black. Because the bed and chairs and pictures and walls are black, it is impossible to find her black cat! Children will love how she solves her dilemma with the magic of color.

**Suggestion**: Read the story while wearing a witch's costume. Children could make a large poster of her new, colorful house!

*Mouse Paint* is a good lead in for Group 2 colors because it is a story about three white mice and how they discover the primary colors red, blue, and yellow.

*White is the Moon* is another collection of poems that describe the nature of colors with artistic pictures that will invite children to explore the wide variety of each color.

## Group 2: *"What Is Red?" "What Is Blue?" "What Is Yellow?"*

*Who Said Red?* is perfect for choral reading. It begins by asking "Who said red?" and introduces blue, yellow, green, purple, and orange in a rhythmic way.

*Little Blue and Little Yellow* is an adventure story where the characters are pieces of torn colored paper.

**Suggestion**: Have the children make characters out of blue and yellow torn paper and create an adventure of their own.

## Group 3: *"What Is Green?" "What Is Orange?" "What Is Purple?"*

*Harold and the Purple Crayon* will have the children wanting to see what they can create with a purple crayon. This is a whimsical story.

**Suggestion**: After reading the story, have the children draw a picture in purple only. When they finish, discuss how they felt making everything in one color. Have pre-cut sheets of purple construction paper ready for mounting; and, if possible, let children snack on grapes while they are enjoying this activity.

## Group 4: *"What Is Brown?""What Is Gold?" "What Is Pink?"*

Read *Brown Bear, Brown Bear, What Do You See?* The title repeats itself throughout the story of the brown bear. After reading the story, older children may read parts of it as the book is passed around.

Read several different versions of *Goldilocks and the Three Bears*. Have students discuss the differences and similiarities between the books.

 

# Journal Writing

**Introduction**: Jessica Jenkins has written a wonderful book about colors and feelings called *Thinking About Colors* (see bibliography page 79). Use this book along with *Rainbows and Frogs* to help children explore how colors can be identified with certain feelings. There are many sayings that relate to colors as well. Feelings about colors make great topics for journal writing. Have the children keep a journal during the unit on colors. Pages are provided for journal writing on these colors: red, blue, yellow, green, orange, purple, gold, and pink. (See pages 36-39.) When the unit is completed, children can make a book out of their writing. Have them design a cover that reflects what they have learned about colors and emotions.

Here are some discussion ideas to use before journal writing assignments:

## Red

* Red can mean anger, bravery, emergencies, and the word "stop."
* People sometimes get a red face when they feel embarrassed.
* "Was my face red!" is a popular saying.

## Blue

* Blue can mean cool, distant, beautiful, and quiet.
* Feeling low or down is described as "feeling blue."
* People who are lonely say they are blue.

## Yellow

* Yellow is connected with brightness and the feelings of fun.
* The color of happiness is yellow.
* "Follow the yellow brick road" is associated with achieving goals.

## Green

* Green is associated with new beginnings, sprouting, or newness.
* "Turning green" means not feeling well.
* "Green with envy" uses green to convey jealousy.

## Orange

* Orange is thought of as the wildest and boldest color.
* Feeling fiery and brave are emotions associated with the color orange.
* Orange can feel fresh like the fruit.

## Purple

* Feeling purple can mean feeling put out or in a pout.
* "In a jam!" is purple.
* Purple can cast a spell.

## Pink

* "In the pink" means feeling healthy.
* Pink feels soft and lovely.
* Newborn and fresh all feel like pink.

## Gold

* Gold is a feeling of royalty like being a king or queen.
* Gold feels like sunshine.
* Bold, strong, solid, and real feel like gold.

# Journal Writing

Red can mean anger, embarrassment, or to stop. How does red make you feel?

Blue is icy or cold. It can also mean sad or lonely. Tell about a time you felt blue.

# Journal Writing *(cont.)*

Yellow is the color of fun and happiness. By following the yellow brick road you are achieving your goals. Write about your goals.

Green describes feeling sick or being envious. What are some good feelings connected with the color green?

# Journal Writing *(cont.)*

Orange is more than a fruit. It is bravery or sunshine. How does orange make you feel?

Purple can make you pout or feel put out. What are some things that make you pout?

 

# Journal Writing *(cont.)*

Gold is regal, gold is solid. Does gold make you feel like you are wearing a crown? Make up a story about what you would do if you were a king or queen.

Pink is a blush or feeling right. If you are in the pink, then you are healthy. What are some things you can do to stay healthy?

# Poetry Pro

Fill in the blanks to create your own color poem. Cut it out and glue it onto a piece of paper. Draw a picture to illustrate your poem. Use the book cover on page 41.

**Example:**

Gold is a sunrise, all shiny and bright.

Gold is a medal.

Gold is a star.

Gold is a mother, who hugs us goodnight.

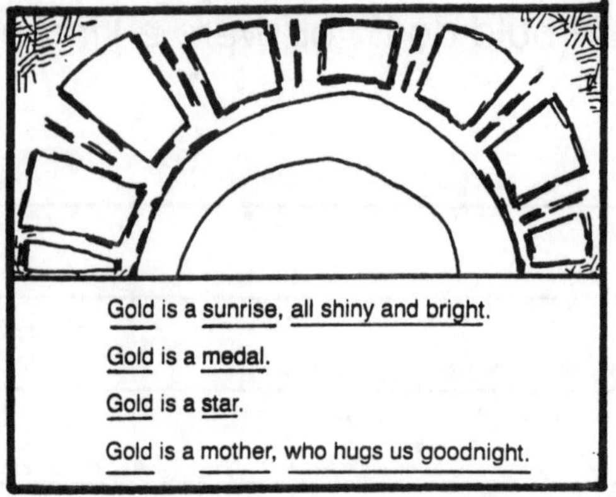


__________ is a ______________, ____________________.
(Color) (Object) (describe the object)

_______ is a ______________.
(Color) (Object)

_______ is a ______________.
(Color) (Object)

__________ is a ______________, ____________________.
(Color) (Object) (describe the object

Name

Name________________________

# Feelings About Colors Survey

People say that colors make them feel warm or cool. Cut squares of blue, red, yellow, green, purple, orange, and pink from construction paper. Show the squares one at a time to at least 4 people. Use tally marks to record which of the four feelings they "feel" from the color (warm, hot, cool, cold).

## Feelings

| Color | Warm | Hot | Cool | Cold |
|---|---|---|---|---|
| BLUE | | | | |
| RED | | | | |
| YELLOW | | | | |
| GREEN | | | | |
| PURPLE | | | | |
| ORANGE | | | | |
| PINK | | | | |

Name ____________________________________

# Graph the Results!

Graph the results here:

| | Warm | Hot | Cool | Cold |
|---|---|---|---|---|
| 10 | | | | |
| 9 | | | | |
| 8 | | | | |
| 7 | | | | |
| 6 | | | | |
| 5 | | | | |
| 4 | | | | |
| 3 | | | | |
| 2 | | | | |
| 1 | | | | |

How many people answered that a color made them feel warm? ____________

How many people answered that a color made them feel hot? ____________

How many people answered that a color made them feel cool? ____________

How many people answered that a color made them feel cold? ____________

**Name** ______________________________

# Color Your Number!

Write your phone number here. ______________________________

Circle the numbers below in the correct order of your telephone number.

| | | | | | | | | | | |
|---|---|---|---|---|---|---|---|---|---|---|
| First digit: | 1 | 2 | 3 | 4 | 5 | 6 | 7 | 8 | 9 | 0 |
| Second digit: | 1 | 2 | 3 | 4 | 5 | 6 | 7 | 8 | 9 | 0 |
| Third digit: | 1 | 2 | 3 | 4 | 5 | 6 | 7 | 8 | 9 | 0 |
| Fourth digit: | 1 | 2 | 3 | 4 | 5 | 6 | 7 | 8 | 9 | 0 |
| Fifth digit: | 1 | 2 | 3 | 4 | 5 | 6 | 7 | 8 | 9 | 0 |
| Sixth digit: | 1 | 2 | 3 | 4 | 5 | 6 | 7 | 8 | 9 | 0 |
| Seventh digit: | 1 | 2 | 3 | 4 | 5 | 6 | 7 | 8 | 9 | 0 |

Color each number you circled according to the color code beside the telephone.

**1 Red**
**2 Green**
**3 Yellow**
**4 Blue**
**5 Purple**
**6 Orange**
**7 Black**
**8 Pink**
**9 Brown**
**0 Gray**

# Storytelling

Dear Parent:

As part of our unit on colors, we read a story about a black crow. This is a legend told by the Lenape Native American tribe. The story describes how the Rainbow Crow became black to save all the other animals in the forest.

Storytelling saves interesting tales that might otherwise be lost. Please tell a story with your child. Space is provided for your child to make a drawing or write a description. This will be shared in class.

Thank you for keeping alive the art of storytelling.

**Name** ________________________________

# What's in a Newspaper?

Newspapers give us information. Look at a newspaper and answer these questions:

1. Weather — Find the high temperature in your city.

   Page____High Temperature____

2. Sports — Find the name of an athlete.

   Page____Athlete's name________________

   Sport ________________________________

3. Advertisements — Find something that a person would buy.

   Page____Item ________________________________

4. Comics — Find a comic strip that you like to read.

   Page____Title________________________________

5. Front Page — Find a story on the front page.

   Who/What is it about? ________________________________

   ________________________________

What is your favorite section of the newspaper?

________________________________

________________________________

Name ______________________________

# Uniforms

**Definition of Uniform:**

Dress of the same design worn by members of a particular group serving as a means of identification.

A common color for uniforms is the color blue.

Members of the United States Navy wear uniforms in blue. In Great Britain, the policemen wear dark blue uniforms. Because so many factory workers wear blue uniforms, these workers are often called "blue-collar workers." However, not every uniform is blue.

What color is the uniform for nurses?

______________________________

What color are the uniforms at your favorite fast food restaurant? ______________________________

______________________________

What other jobs can you think of where people wear uniforms to work?

______________________________

**Homework:**

Call a business that has employees who wear uniforms. Tell them you are studying uniforms. Ask about the color(s) of the company's uniform and report your findings to the class.

Business: ______________________________

Description of uniform: ______________________________

______________________________

______________________________

**Name** ______________________________

# What Does Red Cross Mean?

The worldwide symbol of a red cross on a white background signifies cooperative health services as well as First Aid. The Red Cross is an organization that provides many services such as:

Training nurses and public health workers.

Aiding refugees, and flood and earthquake victims.

Teaching first aid, nutrition and child care.

Protecting civilians, wounded soldiers and prisoners during war.

A red cross on the white background is also a symbol for first aid. Color in the red cross.

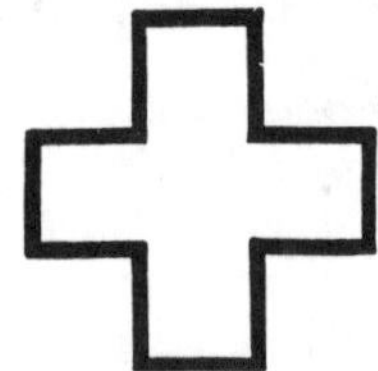

Locate your classroom First Aid kit and make a list of the items in it:

______________ ______________ ______________

______________ ______________ ______________

______________ ______________ ______________

 

Name ______________________________

# Safety and First Aid

First Aid kits are helpful in case of accidents. To avoid accidents, follow the rules of safety. Here are some to remember. Fill in the missing word. Pictures will give you a hint.

1. Never run with______________________ in your hand.
2. Pass scissors with__________________ closed and the handle pointed toward the person.
3. Keep objects with_________________ edges covered and away from small children.
4. When crossing the street, red means ________, yellow means________ and green means________.
5. Wear ___________________ clothing if walking on a dark street at night.
6. Be sure to cross the street at the ______________________.
7. In the classroom or at home, always_________________. Don't run!

**Homework:** Make a list of the emergency numbers to keep near the telephone.

## Emergency Numbers

Fire Department ______________________________

Police Department ______________________________

Doctor ______________________________

Hospital ______________________________

Nearest Relative ______________________________

Nearest Neighbor ______________________________

Work number of parents ______________________________

______________________________

______________________________

*Science*
**Name** ______________________________________

# The Blue Sea

The ocean is blue. There are many different kinds of colorful fish and sea animals that live in the sea. Color the picture using the following colors.

| | | |
|---|---|---|
| 1 - pink | 3 - blue-green | 5 - brown |
| 2 - purple | 4 - blue | 6 - green |

# Colorful Ocean Scenes

After students have become familiar with a variety of ocean plant and animal life, have them make a three-dimensional scene. If possible, collect actual objects—shells, coral, kelp, etc. Otherwise, students can cut out shapes from various materials (see list below). Projects can be made individually or in small groups. Encourage students to choose a theme for their ocean scenes.

## Materials

Empty cans (soup, nuts, potato chips, etc.); sandpaper; scissors; rubber cement; construction paper; materials (art tissue, felt, yarn, buttons, shells, sequins, etc.); white glue

## Directions

- Wrap the sandpaper around the can; leave about 1/4 inch (6mm) border for overlapping.
- Cut off the top of the sandpaper so that it is even with the top of the can.
- Apply rubber cement to the entire outer surface of the can and to the back of the sandpaper; allow to dry before attaching to can. (This process is called a dry mount and the adhesion is very strong.)
- Carefully wrap the sandpaper around the can.
- Cut out sea shapes from the various materials.
- Glue to the outside of the can.
- Actual artifacts can also be glued to the outside of the can.

## Extension

- Have students write stories or poems about their finished projects. Place the writings inside the can. Students can read them during free time or have students share their stories in large or small groups.

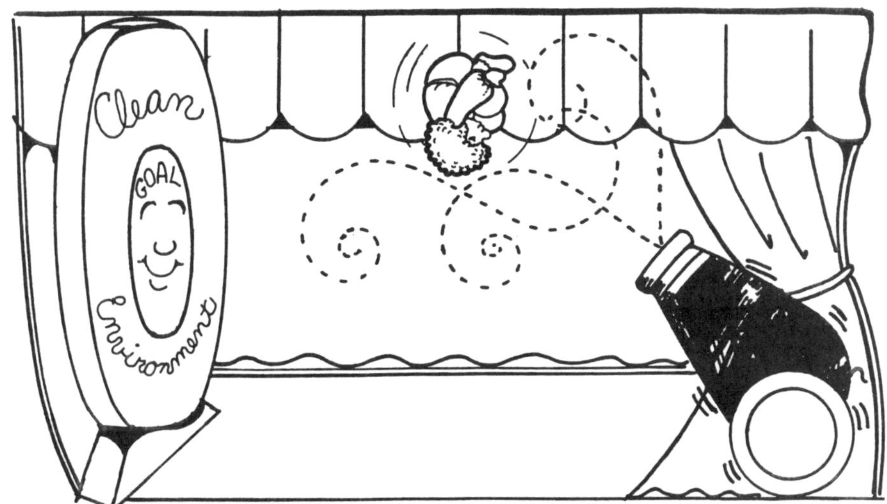

# Air Pollution

What color is the sky on a clear, sunny day? Of course it is blue. Now read some facts about air pollution.

**Facts about Air Pollution:**

1. Air pollution is called smog as a contraction of "smoke" and "fog."
2. Air pollution is composed of hundreds of toxic ingredients such as: carbon monoxide, nitrogen oxide, ozone, and sulphur oxide.
3. Power plants expel large amounts of pollutants.
4. Small businesses such as dry cleaners and auto body shops must be careful with pollutants.
5. Car exhaust contributes 2/3 of the air pollution.
6. Hair sprays, deodorants, and room fresheners in aerosol cans expel small amounts of gases into the atmosphere.

Air pollution caused by all these things can make the sky look muddy or smoky gray.

## Do you have a solution to pollution?

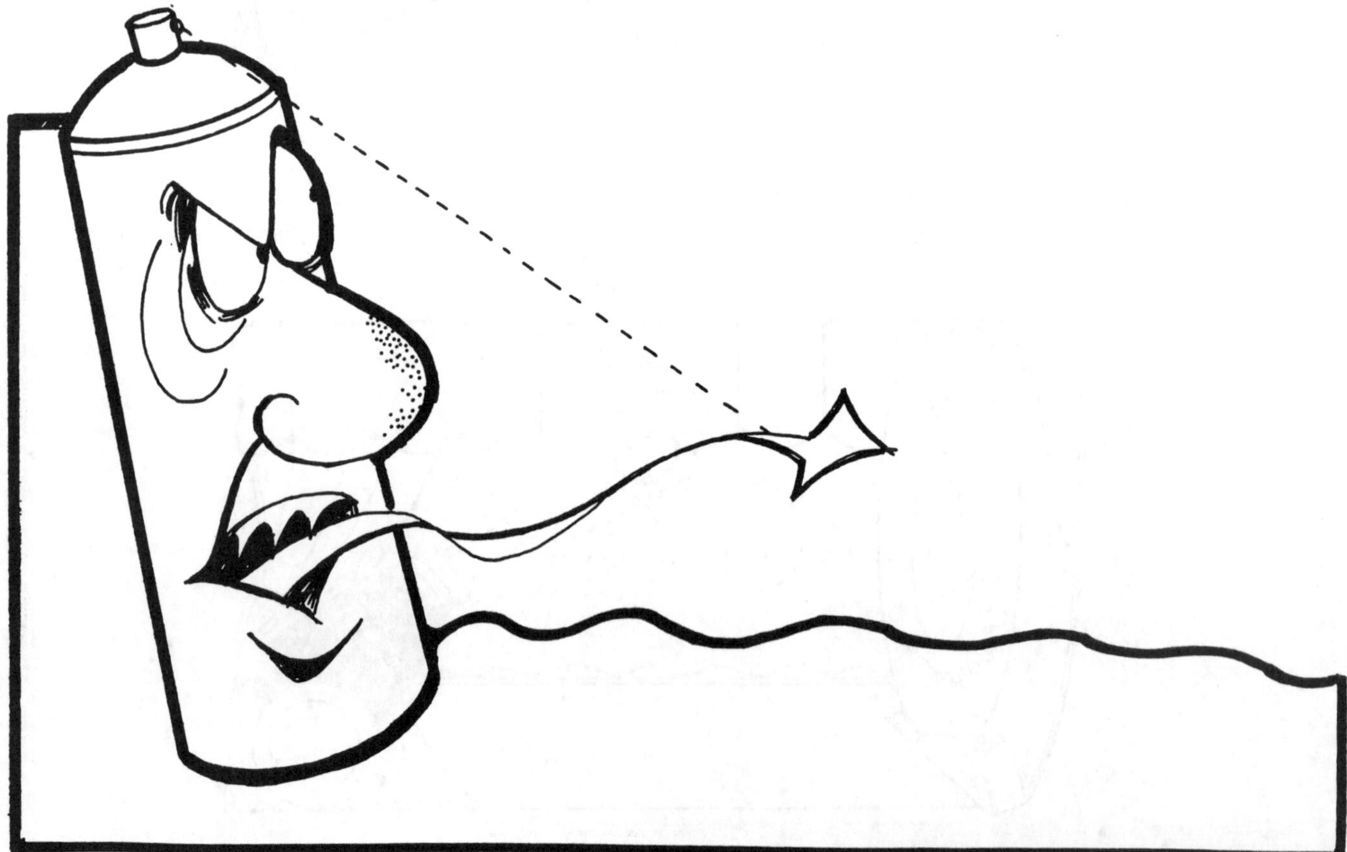

 

# Air Pollution *(cont.)*

What can you do to help keep the sky blue? Here are some ideas to help cut down on air pollution.

* Ask family and friends to use water-based paints. Remind them to look for auto paints, engine cleaners and other automotive products that are free of chlorofluorocarbons.

* Take an inventory of household items. Check for pump-type sprays instead of aerosol cans.

* Walk or ride bicycles whenever possible. Remind adults to carpool.

With a group, name many different ways to help the pollution problem. Write or draw about one of them in the space below.

**Signed** ________________________________ **Date** ____________

# Hidden Pollution

Color the picture below. You will find two common causes of pollution. Write them here.

_______________________________ _______________________________

Name ________________________________________

# Color Mixing

**Materials:**

2 colors of primary color tempera paints (red, blue, or yellow); 2 brushes

**Directions:**

1. Dip clean brush in one color paint and fill in circles #1 and #3.
2. Dip clean brush in another color paint and fill in circles #2 and #3.
3. What color is circle #3? ________________________________________

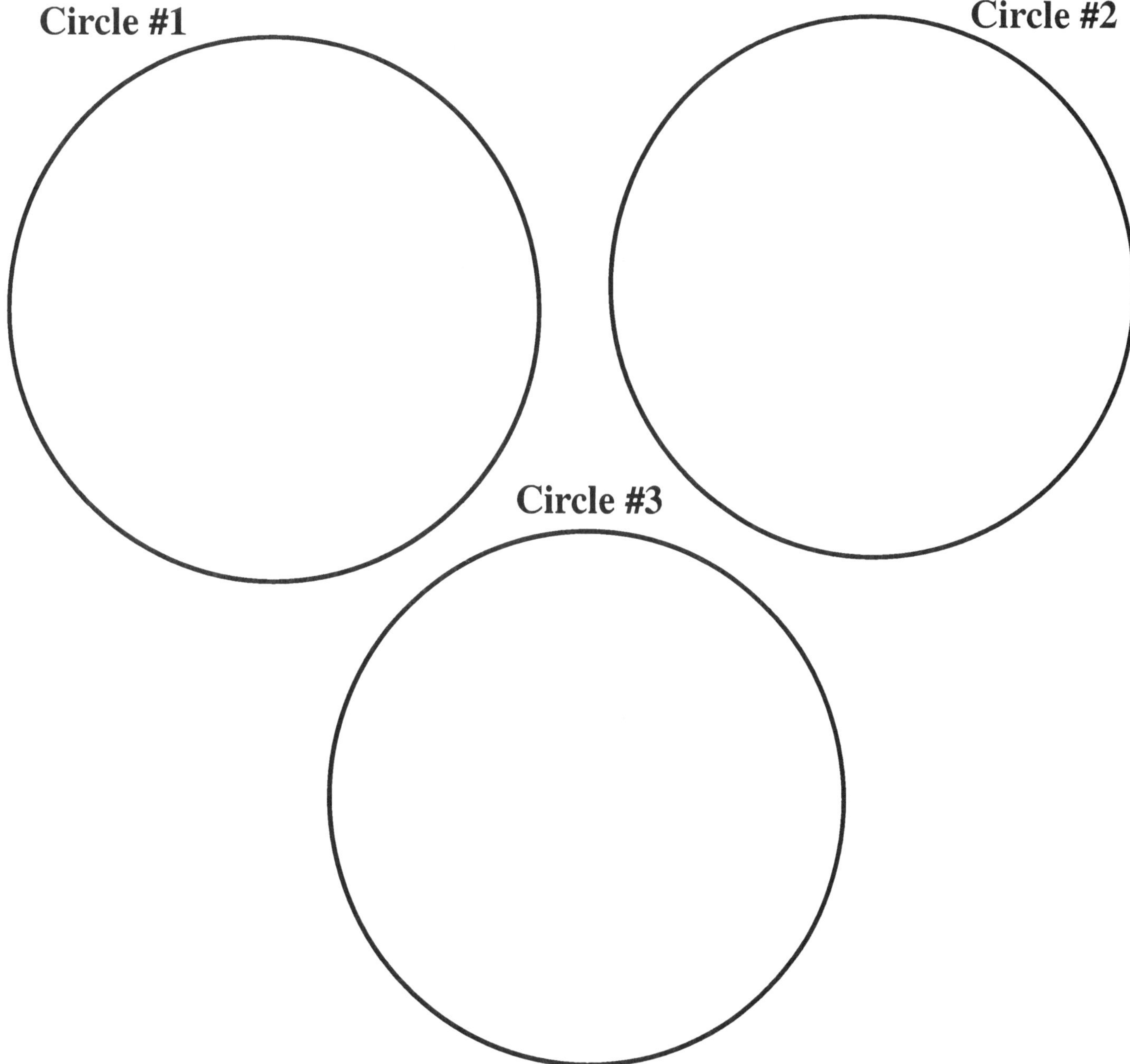


 

# Make a Color Wheel

**Materials:**

- a color wheel
- tempera paints
- brushes

**Directions:**

1. Paint the pieces of the pie with the primary colors: red, blue, and yellow.
2. Mix red and blue, then paint it in the purple part of the color wheel.
3. Mix red and yellow, then paint it in the orange part of the color wheel.
4. Mix blue and yellow, then paint it in the green part of the color wheel.
5. Color wheel is complete.

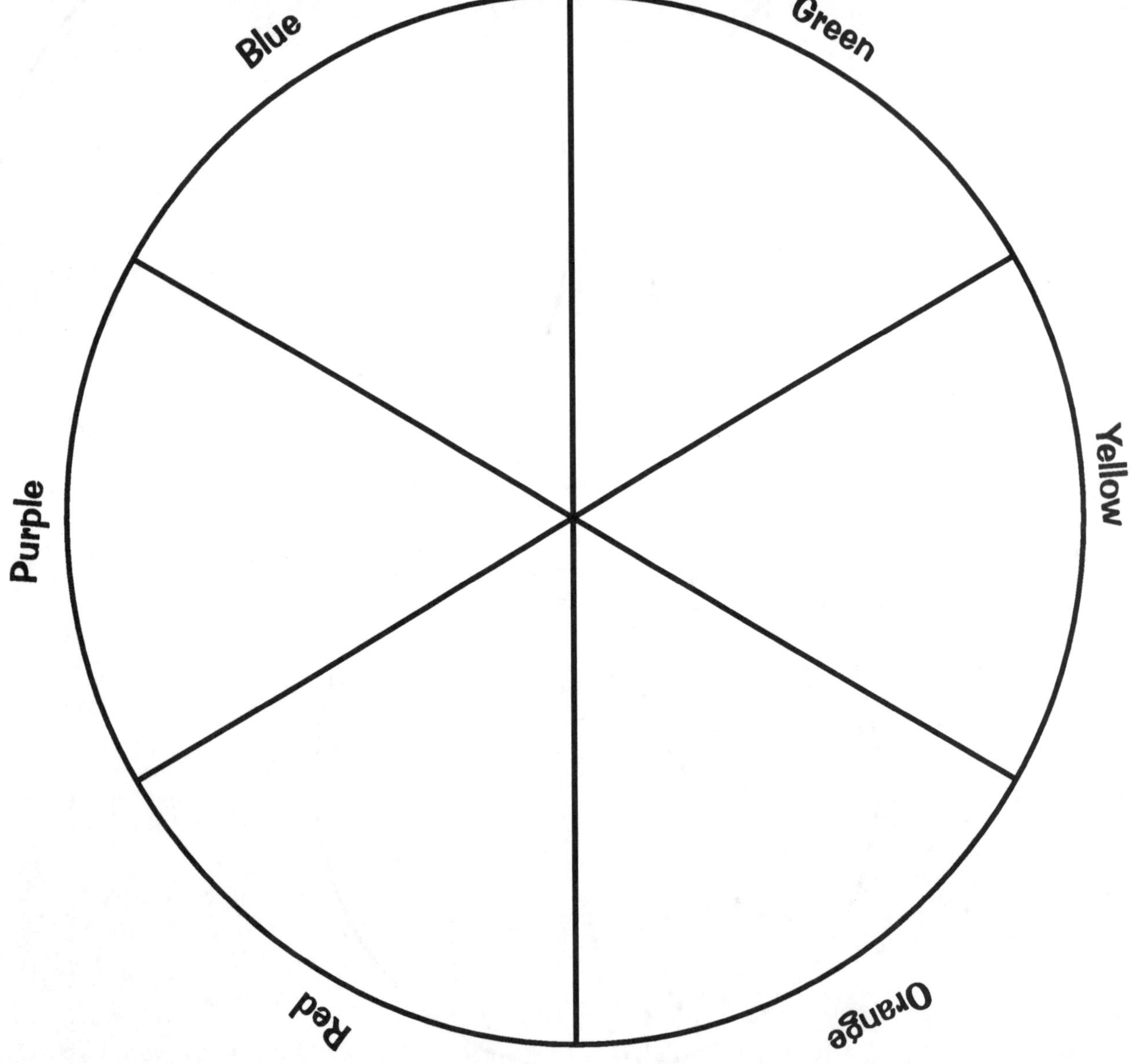


 

# Yarn Art

## Dyeing Yarn

### Materials:

- white yarn
- glass jars or clear plastic cups
- different colors of food coloring
- water

### Directions:

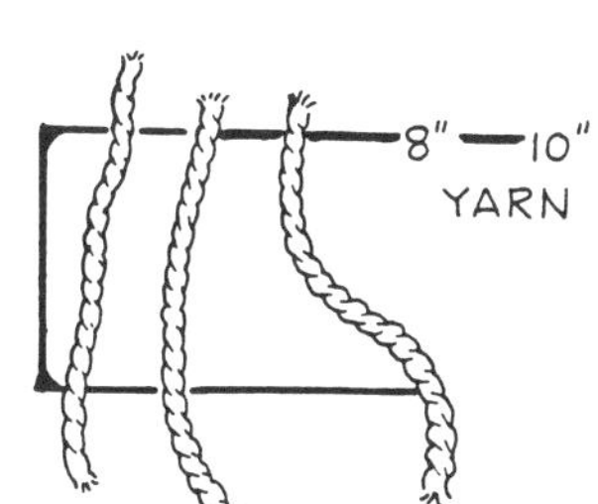


1. Put a few drops of food coloring in containers.
2. Add water and stir.
3. Cut yarn into 8"-10" (20-25 cm) lengths.
4. Give each child three strands of yarn.
5. Have them dip the yarn pieces in the colors of their choice.
6. Place each child's yarn pieces on separate sheets of paper to dry.

## Yarn Bracelets

1. When the yarn has dried, tie the three pieces together at one end.
2. Working in pairs, have one child hold the end while the other braids the yarn.
3. Knot the end.
4. Tie the bracelet around the wrist for a real "handmade" bracelet.

## Yarn Decor

### Materials:

- 1 small balloon for each child
- liquid starch
- glue
- styrofoam food trays
- colored pieces of yarn in different lengths

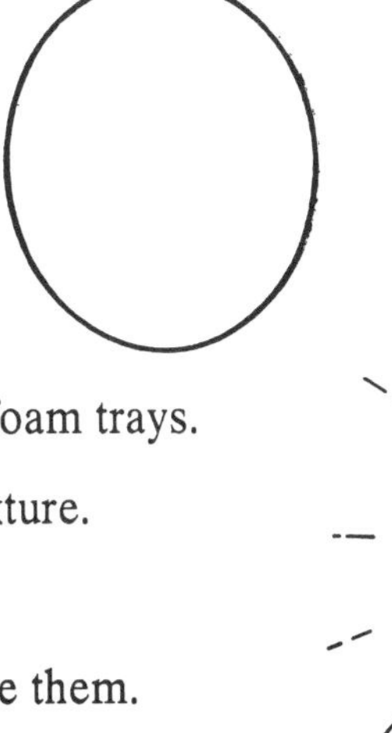

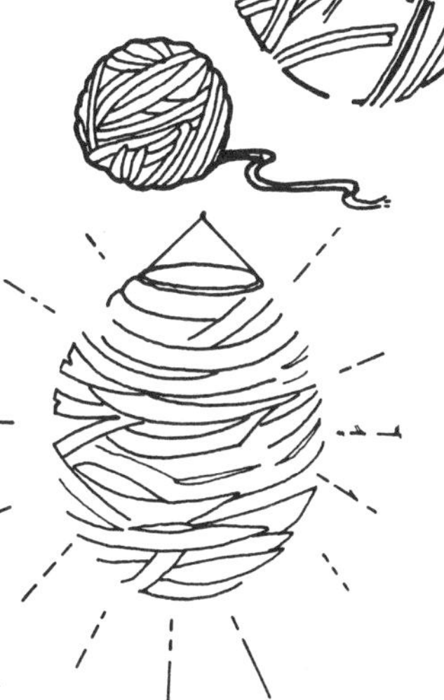

### Directions:

1. Mix equal parts of starch and glue in the styrofoam trays.
2. Have children dip yarn pieces in the liquid mixture.
3. Wrap the yarn around the balloon.
4. Let dry. Pop the balloons and carefully remove them.
5. Hang from the ceiling like Chinese lanterns.

# Physically Fun Activities

The study of colors can be reinforced with activities and games outside the classroom. In addition to being physically fun, these activities are designed to improve listening skills and the following of directions. Once you have taught the children these games, they will ask for them often. Enjoy!

## Word Scramble Run

### Materials

Cut out two sets of individual letters for the words black, white, and gray from corresponding construction paper.

**How to Play:**

1. Line the children up in two groups.
2. Place a set of the letters for black, white, and gray on the ground in front of each line.
3. Place a cone or other type of marker opposite each team. (Determine the distance by the fitness level.)
4. When the whistle blows, the first child in each group picks a letter and runs to the designated spot. The next one in each line picks a letter and runs to the place where the letter fits.

For example: If "W" is picked and then an "E," the second one would leave enough space for the other three letters in the word "WHITE." For duplicate letters such as the "A," the child may choose either word.

5. The team who spells all three words first is the winner.
6. As a variation change the order of the words or use different color words.

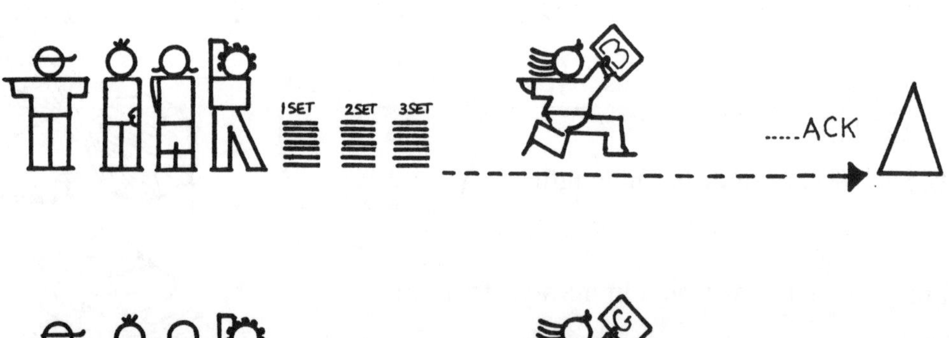


 

# Physically Fun Activities *(cont.)*

## Popcorn Game

### Materials

- 2 parachutes (fabric may be sewn together to make a circle 8 feet or 24 meters in diameter)
- 24 styrofoam balls (2" diameter or 50 mm)

### Directions:

Spray paint the styrofoam balls, 8 each in red, blue and yellow.

### How to Play:

1. Divide the children into two groups.
2. Place them evenly around each parachute.
3. Have them grip the parachute around the edges.
4. For warm-up, have them shake the parachute vigorously.
5. To play the game, place 12 styrofoam balls on each parachute.
6. First team to shake the parachute until all the balls bounce off and onto the ground wins the game.

## Balloon Volleyball

### Materials

- Yarn or string
- Inflated balloons: green, orange, and purple

### Directions

Use yarn to make a "net" by tying it to two chairs or something else that will hold it.

If there is a rug area for children to sit, put yarn 3' (90 cm) from the floor.

If they are at their seats, put yarn 5' (150 cm) high.

### How to Play:

1. This is an informal game with children trying to bat the balloon back and forth across the yarn.
2. Two balloons may be used at a time for variation.
3. Scoring is done when one side fails to return the ball.
4. The balloon can be batted as many times as necessary to return over the yarn.

# Physically Fun Activities *(cont.)*

## Scarf Juggling

### Materials

- 12" (30 cm) squares of fabric in brown, gold, and pink

### Directions

Give each child a set of three scarves. Teach them how to hold the scarves in the center. Extend the arm over the head and toss it in the air. Catch the scarf at waist level.

### How to Play

1. Give verbal cues (call out a color) for which scarf is to be tossed in the air and caught.
2. Call out colors in a rhythmic timing.
3. See who can "juggle" the scarves the longest!

## Stardom!

### Materials

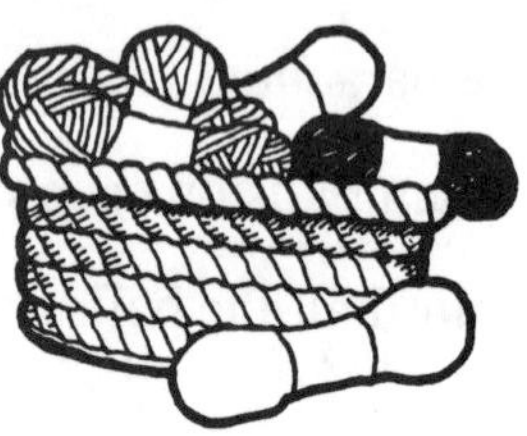
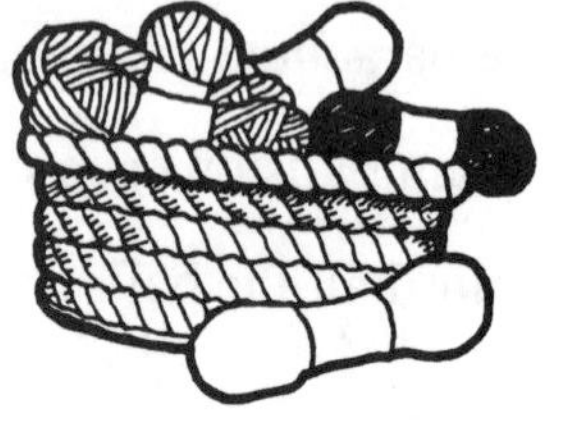

- Skeins of yarn in different colors

### How to Play

1. After children have practiced making stars on paper (see page 61), divide them into five groups.
2. Line them up according to the diagram at the right. Have them face inward.
3. Begin with #1 and have that child hold one end of the yarn while tossing the yarn to #2, across to #3, over to #4, down to #5, and back to #1.
4. Rotate the lines.
5. Repeat with different colors of yarn.
6. Children will love creating the big, soft, fuzzy star!

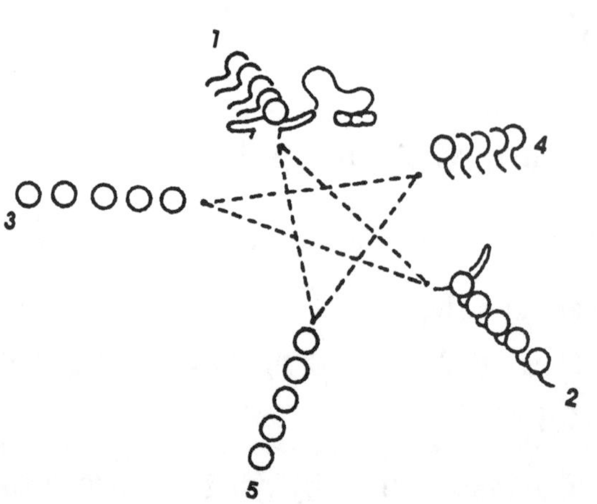


**Variation**: As a certain color of yarn is being tossed, have children call out the names of things that color.

**Reminder**: Be sure to have the camera ready when the star is finished!

 

Name ___________________________________

# Yarn Stars

**Directions:** Practice making yarn stars before making a BIG one outside. Color the stars when all the dots are connected.

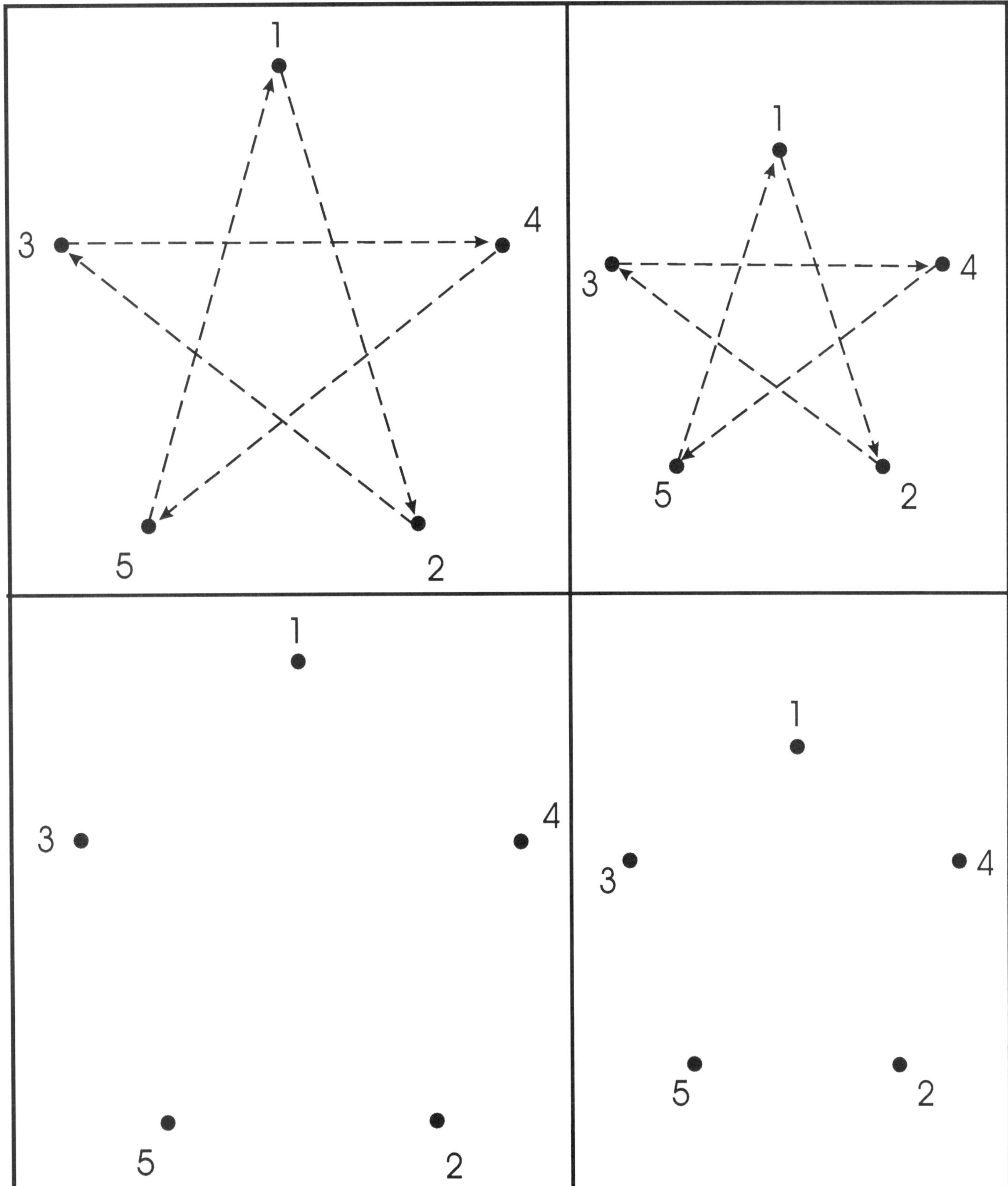

# Foods with Color

## Making Butter

- Empty baby food jars
- Whipping cream

Two children can take turns shaking a baby food jar half filled with whipping cream. Make sure the jar is shaken vigorously for at least 6 minutes. Lumps of yellow butter will form. Rinse off the liquid and butter.

## Corn Feast

Corn on the cob can be a fun experience for children. Demonstrate removing the husks before the children try it. Several children can work on the same cob. Cut the corn in half or thirds before heating in boiling water. Serve on paper plates with butter.

## Snack Ideas

## Peanut Butter and Honey Squares

- wheat bread
- honey
- peanut butter

Cut each slice of bread into four square pieces. Spread with peanut butter and top with honey. Arrange on a tray covered with pink paper or a pink placemat.

For table decorations, set vases with pink carnations on the table and use pink napkins for serving. Bon appetit!

## Red, White, and Blue Parfaits

- cherry gelatin
- blueberry gelatin
- whipped cream

Prepare the cherry and blueberry gelatins (keep separate). After the gelatin has set, spoon a layer of the blueberry gelatin into a clear plastic cup or glass. Add a layer of whipped cream. Top with a layer of cherry gelatin. Enjoy!

 

# Colorful Celebrations Across the Curriculum

To complete the unit on color, additional activities are suggested in Language Arts, Science, and Social Studies that celebrate color. The final activity will be a "Colorful Celebration" for family and friends to share in the fun. See page 70 for guidelines.

## Language Arts

Begin by reading *Beside the Bay* by Sheila White Samton. This is the story of a walk around the bay. It is an opportunity for you to discuss with the children the art of observation. Lead a discussion with these questions: What does observation mean? What senses are used for good observation? Does color make a difference?

Following the discussion, have the children work with a partner. Ask one child to describe to the other child something in the classroom. They are to describe it in detail. The other child has to guess what is being described. Then they switch roles. This will prepare the children for the "Parade of Color" activity.

For the "Parade of Color" activity, take children on a walk around the school or neighborhood. If possible, carry a Polaroid camera to capture the "scene" each child wants to report on.

Return to the classroom and hand out the activity sheet on page 65. Tell the children that they are to pretend they are newspaper reporters. Have them draw the picture of something they saw. Below it, they are to write an "article" as if it were going in a newspaper. These can be displayed on a bulletin board. Title the board "Parade of Color."

## Social Studies

There are several books that show the importance of color in celebrations around the world. *Hawaii is a Rainbow* and *All the Colors of the Race* (see Bibliography page 79) can be used to introduce children to the world of color in many cultural celebrations. Holidays and festivals are celebrated throughout the world. Every country has customs and traditions. Even in our 50 states there are special events and foods not as common in the other states. Work together to match the paragraphs about celebrations in Japan, Hawaii, Vietnam, India, Germany, and Alaska with the pictures. Have students cut out the pictures and glue them next to the celebration. On pages 66-67 read the descriptions of activities that happen during different celebrations. Ask the children to identify the colors.

| | |
|---|---|
| **Japan** | Cherry blossoms are pink or white. |
| **Hawaii** | Flower leis come in many colors; lavender, white, yellow, and red are the most popular colors. |
| **Vietnam** | Brightly colored lanterns can be any color. |
| **India** | Festival of lights will be yellow from the flames. |
| **Germany** | Green wreaths with red candles are traditional Christmas colors. |
| **Alaska** | Mukluks are boots that are usually brown in color. |

Have the children complete the worksheet.

# Colorful Celebrations *(cont.)*

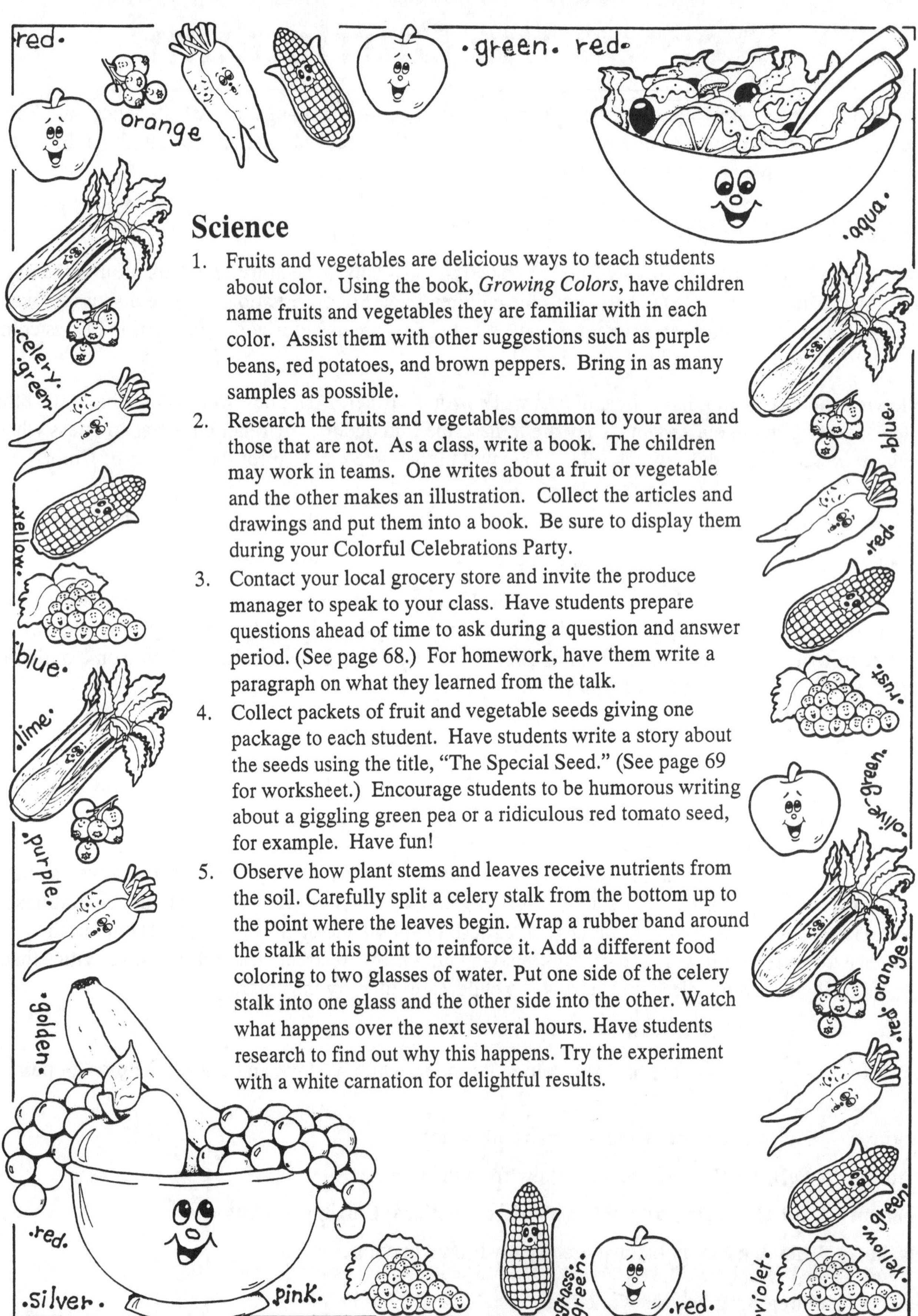


## Science

1. Fruits and vegetables are delicious ways to teach students about color. Using the book, *Growing Colors*, have children name fruits and vegetables they are familiar with in each color. Assist them with other suggestions such as purple beans, red potatoes, and brown peppers. Bring in as many samples as possible.
2. Research the fruits and vegetables common to your area and those that are not. As a class, write a book. The children may work in teams. One writes about a fruit or vegetable and the other makes an illustration. Collect the articles and drawings and put them into a book. Be sure to display them during your Colorful Celebrations Party.
3. Contact your local grocery store and invite the produce manager to speak to your class. Have students prepare questions ahead of time to ask during a question and answer period. (See page 68.) For homework, have them write a paragraph on what they learned from the talk.
4. Collect packets of fruit and vegetable seeds giving one package to each student. Have students write a story about the seeds using the title, "The Special Seed." (See page 69 for worksheet.) Encourage students to be humorous writing about a giggling green pea or a ridiculous red tomato seed, for example. Have fun!
5. Observe how plant stems and leaves receive nutrients from the soil. Carefully split a celery stalk from the bottom up to the point where the leaves begin. Wrap a rubber band around the stalk at this point to reinforce it. Add a different food coloring to two glasses of water. Put one side of the celery stalk into one glass and the other side into the other. Watch what happens over the next several hours. Have students research to find out why this happens. Try the experiment with a white carnation for delightful results.

 

# Parade of Color

After a walk around your school or neighborhood, make a drawing and write a description of something of interest as if it were going to be printed in the newspaper.

# Cultural Celebrations

See page 63 for directions.

Spring is a happy time for children in Japan. Doll's Festival falls on March 3 and the girls invite their friends over for a tea party. Dolls are used to represent the Emperor and the Empress. Pink or white cherry blossoms are the main decoration.

May Day is Lei Day in Hawaii. On May 1 children and adults wear colorful flower leis of lavendar, yellow, and red draped over their shoulders. Leis express the spirit of love and friendship on the Hawaiian islands.

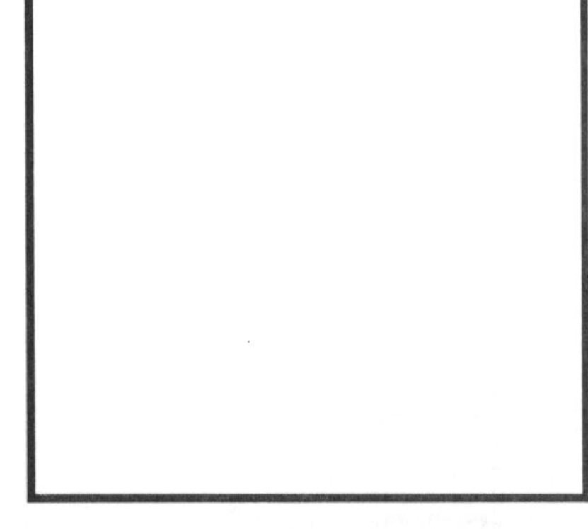

In Vietnam, children love to celebrate Children's Day which takes place during the harvest moon in September. When the day arrives, they help with making moon cakes. These are made with sticky rice and filled with nuts, raisins, and other fruits. In the evening children walk up and down the streets carrying brightly colored paper lanterns. The finale is a dragon parade with lots of dancing and noisy firecrackers.

# Cultural Celebrations

India celebrates Diwali late in October or early November. The "festival of lights" is magical and the children get very excited. They wake up early, take perfumed baths, hang garlands of flowers in the doorways of their homes and help arrange tiny oil lamps everywhere. When night falls, the lamps are lit, casting yellow shadows in hopes that the goddess Lakshmi will come to their home and bring good luck and prosperity.

Christmas in Germany begins near the end of November. They use Advent calendars for counting the number of days until Christmas. Advent wreaths hold four red candles which are lit for each of the four Sundays before Christmas.

In Fairbanks, Alaska, the Native American children celebrate the World Eskimo-Indian Olympics. Arts and crafts are displayed, games are played, and there is a parade and Indian dress contest. The women wear traditional brown boots called mukluks. It is a real authentic celebration.

**Name** ________________________________

# An Interview with the Produce Manager

The Produce Manager is someone in charge of the fruits and vegetables at the grocery store. He/she has assistants to help him/her unload the produce, arrange it in the store and keep it fresh. Think about the questions you would like to ask the Produce Manager. For homework, write a summary of what you learned.

Questions for ________________________________
*(Name)*

1. ________________________________

________________________________

2. ________________________________

________________________________

3. ________________________________

________________________________

4. ________________________________

________________________________

What I learned from ____________________, the Produce Manager:

________________________________

________________________________

________________________________

________________________________

________________________________

________________________________

________________________________

 

# The Special Seed

SEEDS

Fill in the blanks below to create a story about a special seed.

Hi! I am a ______________________ seed. I need three

things to help me grow. They are ____________________,

____________________, and ____________________. The

thing that is special about me is that I can

________________________________________.

The color I will be when I am grown is ________________.

If people eat me, they will be able to

__________________________________________________.

# Colorful Celebrations Party

The children will be excited to share with others the experiences they have enjoyed with colors. To prepare for the celebration party here is a checklist:

## Preparation

- Send out invitations. (see page 78.)
- Complete "Hand-y" bulletin board.
- Finish journal books.
- Hang yarn decor from ceiling.
- Create folders with the following worksheets:

Be a Detective
Colorful Senses
Bullseye
Make a Collage
Compare and Contrast
Color Your Number
Uniforms
First Aid
Picture Math
How Many Blue Eyes?
Colorful Flowers
Hidden Colors
Count the Change
Storytelling
Native Americans
Color Mixing
Math Story
Rhyme Time
History in Color
Word Scramble
Color Survey
What's in a Newspaper?
Red Cross

- Arrange for refreshments using snack ideas from the unit.

fruit assortment; corn on the cob; peanut butter and honey squares; red, white, and blue parfaits (See page 62.)

- Create activity stations for the children to show different projects.

Dyeing yarn
Balloon volleyball
Maypole dancing
Journal Writing
Making newspaper hats
Popcorn game
Book corner
Color wheels
Color Dance
Making butter

On the day of the celebration, the classroom will be vibrant with color. Invite guests to participate in the above activity centers. Make sure children know what they are responsible for and that everyone has an active part.

After everyone has enjoyed themselves and has had a chance to observe the children's work and participate in the activity centers, have everyone seated.

At the conclusion, award each child a Color Specialist certificate found on page 78.

Dear Parents,

Just a note to let you know we are beginning a unit about colors. When we are finished, you will be invited to see the kaleidoscope of activities going on in our room!

______________________________

*Signed*

# "Colors are Hand-y" Bulletin Board

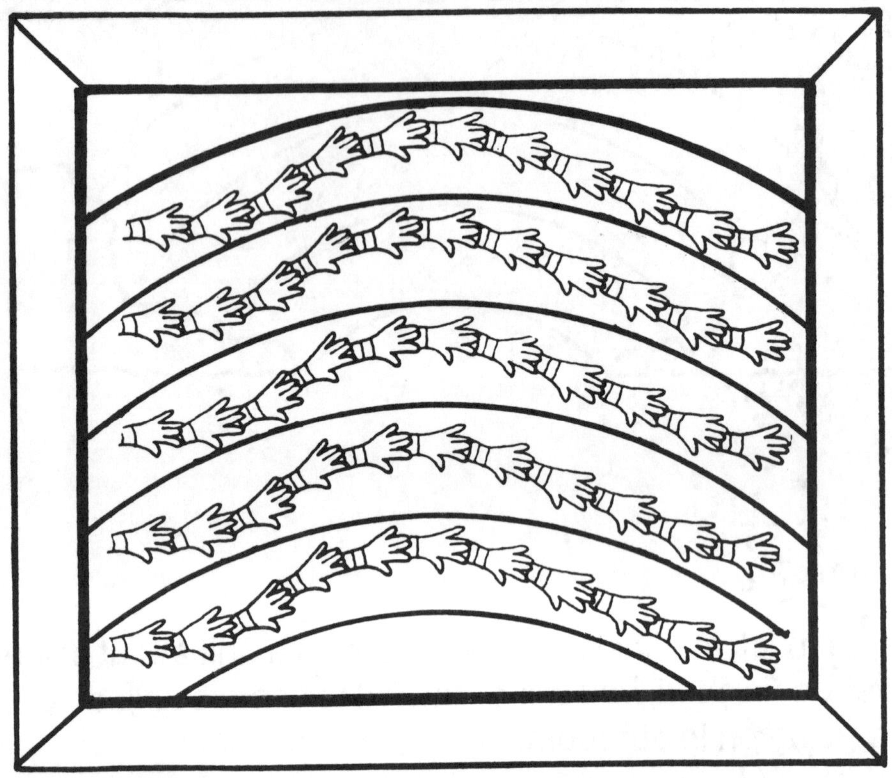

## Objective

This bulletin board allows every child to participate in it 12 times! When finished, there will be no questions how "handy" it is to have color in our world.

## Materials

- White butcher paper
- Tempra paints in each of these colors: black, white, gray, red, blue, yellow, green, orange, purple, brown, gold, and pink
- 12 copies of each child's hand print
- Staples or push pins

## Directions

- Cut out letters or use pre-cut letters for the title, "Colors Are Hand-y."
- During the study of each group of colors, have students make a hand print for each color:

  **Group 1** - black, white, gray
  **Group 2** - red, blue, yellow
  **Group 3** - green, orange, purple
  **Group 4** - brown, gold, pink

- Have children cut out their hand print. For smaller children, prints could be sent home for an adult to cut out.
- Arrange in an arch beginning with Group 1 followed by groups 2, 3 and 4. The children will love watching the rainbow grow!

 

# Classroom Fun!

Colors can be used in many ways during this unit. Here are some suggestions for activities you can include as you read each of the poems.

## Color Clothing Days

There are twelve poems about colors in *Hailstones and Halibut Bones*. For each group, have the children wear clothing that is predominantly one or all three of the colors being studied.

**Group 1:** Black, white, and gray clothing

**Group 2:** Red, blue, and yellow clothing

**Group 3:** Green, orange, and purple clothing

**Group 4:** Brown, gold, and pink clothing

Ways to use the color groups:

- Dismissal
- Monitors
- Teams for physically fun activities

## Exercise Breaks with Color Cards

Make large placards (11" x 17" or 27.5 x 42.5 cm) for each of the 12 colors.

Here is a list of exercise breaks each placard represents:

**Black** Stand up and stretch.

**White** Wave hands in the air.

**Gray** Shrug shoulders.

**Red** Stop what you are doing.

**Blue** Put head down and rest.

**Yellow** Smile.

**Green** Pat on the back.

**Orange** Look from side to side.

**Purple** Touch toes.

**Brown** Tap feet.

**Gold** Shake hands with neighbor.

**Pink** Close eyes, touch nose.

Use the placards during the day. Recognize those children who notice quickly and remember what exercise they are to do.

# Classroom Management Program

Following your unit on colors, here is an excellent classroom management program that uses colors to help designate behavior levels. It provides a visual tool to determine how each child is behaving throughout the day. Here is how it works:

- Using the pattern on page 76 cut out a set of stars for each child. A set consists of one gold, green, orange, red, and blue star. Any color combination will work.
- On a bulletin board, measure the space needed for each child's set of stars. Arrange nails or sturdy push pins accordingly.
- Place a set of stars on each nail and label underneath with each child's name.
- Reproduce the 25 cent money slips on green and cut out. See pattern on page 76.

You are ready to proceed with the program.

1. If you have established expectations, review them with the class. Following are some suggested positive behavior expectations:
   - Follow all directions.
   - Stay on task and complete all assignments on time.
   - Keep hands, feet, and objects to oneself.
   - Work independently.
   - Raise hand and wait to be called on before talking.
   - Treat everyone with respect and kindness.
2. Each student begins the day with a gold star. There is a motivation for keeping the gold star all day.
3. If a student does not follow one of the class rules, the student is told to change the color of their star. This can be done anytime throughout the day including times out of the classroom such as assemblies, library visits, or P.E.
4. When a student changes the color of his/her star, the consequences are as follows:

   **Orange Star** Warning only!

   **Green Star** Child takes time out for 10 minutes in designated area.

   **Red Star** Child meets with teacher during acceptable time and discusses the behavior and ways to change.

   **Blue Star** Child meets with teacher; and, after discussion about the unacceptable behavior, a consultation letter is sent home and parents are requested to sign it. Use a pre-designed checklist.
5. Reinforcements are for both the individual child and the class.

 

# Classroom Management Program *(cont.)*

## Individual Incentive

Each day a student may earn $.25 (green slips) for having homework ready to be checked first thing in the morning AND keeping his/her gold star for behavior. A diagonal mark indicates his/her homework is complete. (/) At the end of the day, those with gold stars get a diagonal mark in the other direction. (\) See class record form on page 77.

Pick a day each week to pass out the "money" earned. At the end of the quarter, those children earning $7.50 will receive a T-shirt. (These can be funded by recycling or other fund raising activities.) Once they have earned a T-shirt, each quarter thereafter, they are aiming for a star to add to their T-shirt. Children find this a lot more exciting and long lasting than candy!

## Classroom Incentive

To keep the enthusiasm alive, the class is given a star on the board each day five children or less have to change their star color. Stars can be given when certain behaviors are happening that need reinforcement such as quiet or straight lines, excellent team work, everyone doing their homework, and a good job on a particular assignment, just to name a few.

Children will really react when others have to change their stars...and they encourage each other about homework and lines etc. to earn class stars.

When a goal of 15 stars is achieved, the class earns a party which is more than just bringing food and listening to music. Special video programs are shown, picnic lunch in the room, celebration birthdays, and having a balloon release are just some of the events that might happen for a party.

## Another Approach

### Gumball Machine Management

Another type of management program you may wish to use is one that rewards whole class behavior. Using a large sheet of tag board or poster board, make a gumball machine. Have prepared gumballs of several different colors cut from construction paper. Tell the students that when the machine is full, the class will be rewarded. The reward can be an extra recess, party, movie, or anything the students will value.

Tell the students that they may earn up to five gumballs each day. Each color gumball will represent a different positive accomplishment that the whole class has achieved. You may determine what the different colored gumballs will represent or use the guidelines listed below.

| Color | Achievement |
|---|---|
| Red | Everyone completed homework |
| Blue | Everyone lined up quickly and quietly |
| Green | There were no overdue library books |
| Orange | Everyone followed directions |
| Yellow | Everyone respected one another |

Adapt this program to fit the need of your class. You may decide to change the number of gum balls it is possible to earn, or the amount of gumballs that is necessary before the class will earn a reward.

# Pattern/Money Slips

Make two copies of money slips for full page reproducible

| | |
|---|---|
| 25 CENTS<br>A Gold Star to You! | 25 CENTS<br>A Gold Star to You! |
| 25 CENTS<br>A Gold Star to You! | 25 CENTS<br>A Gold Star to You! |
| 25 CENTS<br>A Gold Star to You! | 25 CENTS<br>A Gold Star to You! |

 

# Class Record Form

| Name | | | | | | | | | | | | | | | | | | | | | | |
|---|---|---|---|---|---|---|---|---|---|---|---|---|---|---|---|---|---|---|---|---|---|---|
| | | | | | | | | | | | | | | | | | | | | | | |
| | | | | | | | | | | | | | | | | | | | | | | |
| | | | | | | | | | | | | | | | | | | | | | | |
| | | | | | | | | | | | | | | | | | | | | | | |
| | | | | | | | | | | | | | | | | | | | | | | |
| | | | | | | | | | | | | | | | | | | | | | | |
| | | | | | | | | | | | | | | | | | | | | | | |
| | | | | | | | | | | | | | | | | | | | | | | |
| | | | | | | | | | | | | | | | | | | | | | | |
| | | | | | | | | | | | | | | | | | | | | | | |
| | | | | | | | | | | | | | | | | | | | | | | |
| | | | | | | | | | | | | | | | | | | | | | | |
| | | | | | | | | | | | | | | | | | | | | | | |
| | | | | | | | | | | | | | | | | | | | | | | |
| | | | | | | | | | | | | | | | | | | | | | | |
| | | | | | | | | | | | | | | | | | | | | | | |
| | | | | | | | | | | | | | | | | | | | | | | |
| | | | | | | | | | | | | | | | | | | | | | | |
| | | | | | | | | | | | | | | | | | | | | | | |
| | | | | | | | | | | | | | | | | | | | | | | |
| | | | | | | | | | | | | | | | | | | | | | | |
| | | | | | | | | | | | | | | | | | | | | | | |
| | | | | | | | | | | | | | | | | | | | | | | |
| | | | | | | | | | | | | | | | | | | | | | | |
| | | | | | | | | | | | | | | | | | | | | | | |
| | | | | | | | | | | | | | | | | | | | | | | |
| | | | | | | | | | | | | | | | | | | | | | | |
| | | | | | | | | | | | | | | | | | | | | | | |
| | | | | | | | | | | | | | | | | | | | | | | |
| | | | | | | | | | | | | | | | | | | | | | | |

# Awards

**You Are Invited to a**

## Colorful Celebration Party!

**When:**

**Where:**

**Time:**

***We're counting on you, that's definitely true.***

***So please let us know you will be here, too!***

**will attend** ______________

**will not attend** ______________

______________________________
*signed*

## Color

### Specialist Award

**presented to**

______________________________

______________________________
*signed*

______________________________
*date*

 

# Bibliography


Adoff, Arnold. ***All Colors of the Race.*** Morrow/Beech Tree, 1982.

Adoff, Arnold. ***Greens***. Lothrop, 1988.

Aliki. ***How a Book Is Made***. Harper & Row, 1986.

Ardley, Neil. ***The Science Book of Color.*** Harcourt, Brace, Jovanovich, 1991.

Ehlert, Lois. ***Color Farm.*** Harper Collins, 1990.

Ehlert, Lois. ***Color Zoo***. Harper Collins, 1990.

Ehlert, Lois. ***Planting a Rainbow.*** Harcourt, Brace, Jovanovich, 1988.

Feeney, Stephanie. ***Hawaii is a Rainbow.*** University of Hawaii Press, 1985.

Greeley, Valerie. ***White is the Moon***. MacMillan Publishing Company, 1990.

Hoban, Tana. ***Is It Red? Is It Yellow? Is It Blue?*** Greenwillow Books, 1978.

Jenkins, Jessica. ***Thinking About Colors***. Dutton Children's Books, 1992.

Johnson, Crockett. ***Harold and the Purple Crayon.*** Harper & Row, 1989.

Jonas, Ann. ***Color Dance.*** Greenwillow Books, 1989.

Kim, Joy. ***Rainbows and Frogs.*** Troll Associates, 1981.

Konigsburg, E.L. ***Samuel Todd's Book of Great Colors.*** Atheneum, 1990.

Lionni, Leo. ***Matthew's Dream.*** Alfred A. Knopf, 1991.

Lynn, Sara. Primers ***Colors***. Little, Brown & Company, 1990.

Martin, Bill. ***Brown Bear, Brown Bear What Do You See?*** Henry Holt & Company, 1983.

McMillan, Bruce, ***Growing Colors.*** Lothrop, Lee and Shepard Books, 1988.

O'Neill, Mary. ***Hailstones and Halibut Bones.*** Doubleday & Company, 1961.

Paul, Korky. ***Winnie the Witch***. Kane/Miller, 1987.

Rossetti, Christina. ***Color***. Harper Collins, 1990.

Samton, Sheila White. ***Beside the Bay.*** Lothrop, Lee and Shepard Books, 1988.

Serfozo, Mary. ***Who Said Red?*** Macmillan Publishing Company, 1988.

Van Ellet, Matthew. ***One Yellow Lion***. Dial Books for Young Readers, 1992.

Van Laan, Nancy. ***Rainbow Crow.*** Dragon, 1989.

Walsh, Ellen Stoll. ***Mouse Paint.*** Harcourt, Brace, Jovanovich, 1989.

Warne, Frederick. ***Peter Rabbit's Colors.*** Viking Penguin Inc., 1988.

Woolfit, Gabrielle. ***Colors Red. Colors Blue. Colors Yellow. Colors Green.*** Carolrhoda Books, 1992.

# Answer Key

## Answer Key

**Page 9**

Black: smokestack; charcoal; licorice
White: marshmallow; ship's sails; dove
Gray: mouse; elephant; goats

**Page 10**

shoes; clouds; birds; cats

**Page 11**

1. snowflake
2. mouse
3. blue

**Page 12**

1. sound
2. smell or sight
3. sound
4. smell or sight
5. taste
6. sound
7. taste
8. touch
9. smell, sight or touch

**Page 15**

answers will vary

**Page 16**

Blue: glue, flew, zoo, you, too, few

Red: head, bed, shed, said, fled, dead

Yellow: fellow, mellow, jello, bellow

**Page 17**

1. 2
2. 4
3. 3
4. blue
5. red

**Page 19**

1. white
2. gold
3. red
4. red, white, and blue
5. yellow

**Page 24**

1. black
2. yellow
3. white
4. purple
5. red
6. green
7. orange
8. gray

**Page 49**

1. scissors
2. blades
3. sharp
4. stop; caution; go
5. white or light
6. crosswalk
7. walk

 